Secrets of a Stylish Home

Secrets of a Stylish Home

Cate Burren

Photography by
Simon Whitmore

MERRELL
LONDON · NEW YORK

Introduction

I believe that the purpose of interior-designing a home is to achieve the best possible surroundings for the people who live in it. It is about creating an environment that reflects their personality and taste, that they can feel proud of and feel comfortable in, and that functions properly for them. Over the years I have been lucky enough to work on a wide range of projects, and I have found that although every brief and every home is different, it is possible to apply a similar tried-and-tested approach to each. This is true whether I am working on a grand hall, a hunting lodge, a town house, a farmhouse or even my own home.

A few years ago I started teaching evening classes called 'How to Interior Design your Own Home', aimed at people who wanted to do it themselves, rather than engaging a professional, but who wanted to know how to get it right and how to avoid the various pitfalls along the way. As I thought about what to include in the course, I tried to be as true to my own process as possible, since I believe this is the right way to approach interior design in any home. Interestingly, running these classes opened my eyes to exactly what I do and what the majority of people find difficult or straightforward. However, what struck me most was that although the students' requirements, style and previous experience – not to mention their homes – were very different, the underlying step-by-step approach really is relevant for every design, whoever is undertaking

the work. The idea for this book was developed from those classes, and from my own hands-on experience, and my aim has been to take away some of the mystery of the interior-design process and break it down into comprehensible stages.

This book starts with the idea of identifying your own interior style. This involves deciding what you like, what you don't like, and how you want your home to look, and I explain how not to get distracted from this as you implement your designs. Chapter 2 is about planning how you will live in your home, and making sure the furniture, lighting, storage and flow between rooms are right for the activities you regularly undertake at home. I believe the first two chapters cover the absolute basics of the interior-design process; it is a very rare project that does not involve these stages. Chapter 3 looks at the use of colour in the home. There is always much discussion about colour in any project, and because it has such a huge impact on the results it is vital to get it right. In chapter 4, I show you how to pull together all the elements discussed in the first three chapters into schemes that are ready to be implemented in your home, and how to source your materials. Finally, chapter 5 explains how to manage your project: there is no point in having beautiful design schemes if they cannot be turned into reality, and there are pitfalls to be avoided here, too.

I have tried to ensure that each section of the book applies to every

Contemporary art and sculpture add all the colour that is needed in this modern, neutral setting.

8

project, whether large or small. If you come to a section that you think may not apply to your project, I challenge you to read it and then decide – every space has the potential to be better in every way.

As an example of this, a student renting a room in a shared house came on one of my courses, and I was worried that she might not benefit much from the day. However, it became clear straight away that she not only wanted to understand how to design her own living environment but also was ready to make the absolute best of her room, even though her landlord was opposed to her making changes (even painting the walls). Her final scheme comprised elements of her own style that she had

identified outside the confines of the space she was working with, and had then applied in small but crucial ways to the room. It turned out that the layout and storage could be greatly improved by moving the bed to a different place; better lighting made the room work better and seem larger; and colour was applied cleverly through pictures, bed throws, cushions, a rug and an armchair.

I strongly believe that interior design can make a person feel a connection with their home and feel comfortable in it. Buildings have characters of their own (whether that is spiritual, historical, geographical or spatial – or most likely all of the above), and if we do nothing to engage with a property it will dictate how we live in it. However, if we make an effort to make a mark on the home, to find our own style and learn how to implement it, to define our household's requirements and find how to make them work, it can be a beautiful meeting of minds (yes, a building can have a mind of its own). Most houses last much longer than their inhabitants, and it is important to work with them but not be constrained by their architecture, style, history or layout. Our home is our cave, our nest, our retreat, our theatre and even our confidant. It is the place to which we return, in which we wake up, cry and laugh, and which protects us from the rest of the world; if we respect it, it will be a happy home in which to live, and that is a great benefit to have in life.

Left: This kitchen bay window is matched with a built-in window seat and circular table, creating an attractive spot for informal dining.

Opposite: The rustic furniture in this dining room works particularly well with the neutral colours favoured by the owner.

Finding your style

Whatever your project, finding, developing and understanding your own style is vital to the success of the interior design of your home, and is the most important part of any scheme. Undertaking this process will give you the confidence to make the big, expensive decisions, such as which flooring to select, what kind of art to buy or the best kitchen to choose, as well as the tiny impulsive decisions, such as what flowers should go where, the best table napkins to have and which are the perfect Christmas decorations.

The process may take you a couple of hours or much longer, depending on how well you already know your own personal taste. I always undertake this exercise with my clients, however small the project, and when I move home I start from scratch each time. In my case the outcome is usually slightly different, but you may find that for you the result is exactly the same each time, and that is just as good.

Apply your style to everything

Finding and understanding your own style will influence all your decisions when you decorate your home, from choosing bathroom fittings and lights to placing furniture and accessories, and will also help you to narrow down where to find these items. Time spent becoming sure of your style at the start of a project will prevent upsetting and costly mistakes later.

Find your inspiration

If you don't know exactly what your own style is (and most of us don't at first), start by getting inspiration from magazines, books and real-life sources. Keep a file or a box (or whatever works for you) of pictures of interiors that you like, and try to amass a good handful, even if you don't love everything in every picture. It may help to write down what you really like and anything you dislike about each picture.

Don't let your house dictate your style

Whether you love your home or not, try to think about your own style without reference to the building. The architectural style is important, but unless you know and understand your own style you will not be able to make it work with your home (or indeed any property).

Look at whole rooms

When you are trying to find your own style, it is fine to collect pictures of particular products or pieces of furniture, but you will still need pictures of whole rooms. Identifying a style from only a range of products is quite difficult.

Friends with great houses

If you can identify your own style, you will be free to appreciate and enjoy other people's homes, knowing that their style is different from yours. This ensures that you don't make mistakes by copying things you love about their homes, which may not translate well into your own.

How to identify your style

There are many ways to identify your own style and taste, and it doesn't matter particularly how it is done. We will work through the process in this chapter, and — at the risk of sounding bossy — I am going to say now that this is really important. Don't even think of skipping this chapter, even if you find it difficult. It is infinitely easier to express your style visually than it is to do so in words, so I try to work with imagery, colours, fabrics and objects as much as possible — although I don't discount words.

My first port of call is usually interiors magazines, and I freely tear out any pages that inspire me in some way. When I work with my clients, I take a pile of cuttings showing rooms that I think they will like, but I include a wide enough range that there will be some that they don't like. At this early stage, an image that provokes a strong negative reaction is as useful as an image they love, because it communicates preference and narrows down the looks they want. Often one doesn't understand the reason for a certain reaction to an image, but it doesn't matter; having the reaction is what counts. If you think you don't know what you like, I'm sure you would be able to say what you definitely don't like, so start with that.

The images you collect might not be just pictures of interiors but could also be of places you love or products you desire (a beautiful light or a piece of fabulous furniture), or even art. All these help to build up a picture of your style and preferences. Try to select as many cuttings as you can, and don't stop until you have a good pile of images you genuinely like. This can take a few goes; also, it is useful to look through the pile every so often, as your reaction may change and you may want to get rid of a few of your original choices in favour of others.

It helps to keep the cuttings in an orderly pile somewhere, but at this stage I try not to make up moodboards or to stick anything down. Your ideas should be able to flow and change. A box, tray or folder will allow order without imposing constraints. I have an allocated section in my filing cabinet called 'home inspiration', which sits unglamorously between utility bills and mortgage documents, and, even

When it came to updating this traditional bathroom, the owner wanted to keep the look classic, but to soften the room with warm pink walls and pretty curtains with a glamorous tie-back. The result is beautifully girly.

Opposite: A corner of the main hallway reflects the owner's taste for an elegant, traditional, comfortable family home.

Left: This sculpture of a bird looks magnificent against the backdrop of the country garden.

If you really can't see an obvious pattern, a good exercise is to take some sticky notes or other labels and write down what it is about each picture that you like (or don't like). For example, you may like the flooring, the light and airy feel of a room or the wall colour. In addition, by writing down that you like everything except the sofa/lamp/rug, you may find that you feel more comfortable with your selection. If you still can't see any pattern at all, I suspect you haven't got enough images to work with, and I would suggest doing the exercise again and widening your selection. Even if you are now flagging, please keep going until you have at least a first idea of what your style is. Trust me: it will be worth it.

when my current house is complete, I regularly review and add to this drawer.

Once you have a good selection of cuttings, lay them all out on the table or floor. You will probably start to see a pattern emerging: colours, perhaps, or an overall style, or a propensity to pick out images with certain types of furniture or lighting. You don't need to define these common elements, but noticing them is a big step towards understanding your own style. As you keep working, you will notice that these patterns become clearer, and that you start to see your own taste taking shape. Setting things aside for a few days and looking at it all again with fresh eyes will help. If there are two (or more) of you working on this process, you don't have to agree on everything; keep a pile of 'I like', 'you like' and 'we both like' images, although ideally the 'we both like' pile would grow. Don't worry about trying to pin down a defined style at this point. Your styles will probably develop and change over time, so see this rather as a starting point.

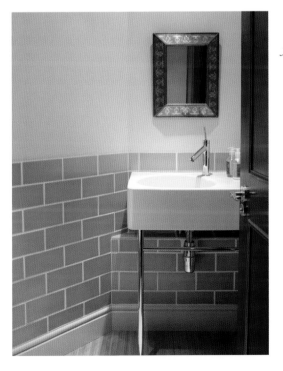

Your style should be applied to all rooms in the house, even your guest cloakroom.

Jenny and Luigi's home style

Jenny is a project manager at my interior-design studio, Angel + Blume, and she and her partner, Luigi, recently bought their first home. Jenny has a well-developed eye for interiors, and when she and Luigi undertook the exercise of evaluating and finding their home style, there were a few surprises but mainly lots of agreement on how they wanted their home to look.

Being highly efficient, Jenny took handfuls of tearsheets that she liked from our studio library, and went through them with Luigi to see what spoke to him and where their tastes overlapped. When she had made a list of images they both liked (which took several attempts), she wrote down on a sticky note what appealed to them about each picture and what didn't, and where they disagreed. She also pulled out six pictures they both loved and felt to embody what they wanted their home to be. What was fascinating (and I think this is true of everyone, even those in the interior-design industry) was that, even having done this, she was still a little unsure of what their style was. When we went through the images and Jenny described what they liked about each picture, very clear ideas emerged and we wrote these down. This list and the selected images were more than enough to give us a clear indication of Jenny and Luigi's style. This does not mean that their house will look like any of these pictures or exactly match the words we used to describe their style, but the process defined how they would select the colours, fabrics, products and accessories that would make up their home.

Some of the tearsheets that Jenny and Luigi originally picked out, with their notes of what they liked and what they didn't.

20

'Like the rustic feel, and the big mirror behind the sink is an interesting idea, although I don't know how it would work in reality.'

'I find this room very inviting. I like the grey colours, and the window is lovely.'

'Love the big windows and the shutters — it feels stylish and comfortable. It is too white for me, and I would prefer some colour.'

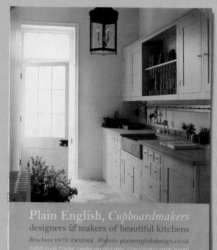

'Love the homely, welcoming Shaker-style kitchen. Like the flooring and the light, airy feel.'

'I love the punch of colour from the yellow curtains against the grey walls. I like the sweeping staircase and the mirror over the door. I don't like the sofa — it doesn't look very comfortable.'

'Like the large family dining table and the pink of the flowers. I am not keen on the pendant lights.'

INDIVIDUAL ITEMS

Do like
✓

Wooden floors

Shutters

Copper pans

Metro wall tiles

Tongue-and-groove panelling

Open shelving

Accent colours

Good bedlinen

Period features, especially deep
   skirting boards

Wooden table and chairs

Reading lights

Panelling

Framed black-and-white pictures

Shaker-style kitchens

Peg rails

Traditional terracotta tiles

Don't like
✗

Very white or dark colours

Plate racks

OVERALL LOOK

Do want
✓

Effortless, casual, relaxed,
   comfortable

Light and airy, calm, textures,
   soft colours with accents
   of colour

Family feel, homely, welcoming

Fairly traditional with quirky
   features, individual

Mix of country and modern,
   a hint of rustic, European

Don't want
✗

Industrial look

Fussiness

Formal

Retro

Anything too modern

CASE STUDY
Kate's home style

Precious possessions sit comfortably with a favourite French conserve – all part of Kate's style.

Kate is also a project manager at my studio, and is an old hand at the property renovation game. She and her young family live in a Victorian house, and, although moving is not on their agenda at the moment, she always has her eye on the property market. Kate has nearly finished her current home and has a good idea of what she likes and dislikes. As an exercise for this book, I asked her to define her style without using tearsheets (although she has a good collection of those already), and so she selected possessions and other items that say something to her. I found the results very interesting, as I think I know her tastes well; they were also revealing to her, as she made several adjustments to her final choice to pinpoint the essence of her style.

It was important not to restrict the number or type of items that Kate used to describe her style, and the furniture, pictures, food and clothing she selected gave a broad visual description of her taste. None of these things have to be part of her home (although many are from her current or previous homes); they simply allow her to use a different language from that of images of interiors to define what she likes.

The items picked out
by Kate to define her
interior style.

WHAT KATE LOVES

❧ The larger of the two artworks has a history in Kate's family, and so is important to her, but she also likes its traditional style and feminine feel, and that it is fluid and doesn't have strong, clean lines. The smaller picture is in fact a framed ceramic tile, and Kate likes the combination of the colours and the sheen of the finish. It shows a little boy and a dog, and the innocence of the subject matter and the naïvety of the artwork appeal to her.

❧ Kate bought the dress at an auction, and for that reason it feels very much like a one-off. Its subtle elegance, glamorous sheen and warm, understated colour caught Kate's eye when she saw it in the sale.

❧ The armchair was given to Kate by a relative, and she likes its traditional shape and the faded glory of the fabric. Kate is attracted to the style of the Bloomsbury Group, found particularly at Charleston, their house in East Sussex, and this chair reminds her of that style.

❧ The rug once belonged to Kate's grandmother, who brought it back from Kuwait. Kate remembers her grandmother's house with its tiled floors and rugs, where she and her brother used to play. Apart from her sentimental attachment to the rug, Kate also likes its warm colours and traditional feel.

❧ The blue enamel bowl, blue-and-white jugs and jar of jam all conjure up images of holidays, markets in France, sunshine and the countryside. Unsurprisingly, these are all visual elements that Kate would not mind living with at home.

❧ The sculpture of a boy's head was a present to Kate's son from his grandfather when he was born. It is important for that reason, and Kate also likes its simplicity, innocence and individuality.

From these pieces, an overall picture of Kate's style emerges: she likes traditional pieces, good naïve art, warm colours, a hint of French country style, some glamour and sheen, an underlying soft, feminine style, individual pieces with history and family memorabilia.

Domestic bliss

One of the questions that came up at one of my recent evening classes was how to handle disagreement in the household (and it seemed to be a popular question, because there was lots of discussion about it). In my experience, it is rare for there to be such a great divide on taste that there is no common ground at all, and — at the risk of being annoying — I believe you may need to embrace each other's styles (rather than compromising) in order to find the right approach. If one householder loves modern and the other traditional, you can combine the elements of each very successfully if each person is prepared to work at it and take into account the interior passions of the other.

It is generally the case that one person is more interested than the other, and wants to involve the other in the process. This is extremely sensible, since the last thing you want is to learn of a strong opinion on something once the purchase has been made. If your other half is not interested at all, try to narrow down your own 'likes' before showing them to your partner, and be open-minded if he or she doesn't automatically agree with you. Sometimes the chance to have a say gets the ball rolling for someone, and that is productive in itself. Also accept that you will most likely be interested in different areas. One person might have strong opinions on how the lighting or radiators should look, and the other might be more

Opposite and above: This kitchen combines exposed traditional brick with a retro-style table and chairs and a modern lamp, all in natural, neutral colours.

Left: Models of seminal modern chair designs sit happily with antique pieces on a Victorian mantelpiece painted in up-to-date neutral colours.

focused on colour or fabrics; so try to work on those areas individually and then see where the overlap is. By going through this process, you should be able to find a style that you both feel happy with, and that should avoid a heated discussion when you come to make key decisions. Just don't say I didn't warn you!

Harmonious home
The couple who own the house pictured on these pages happily mix their styles at home. He is a furniture-maker and a lecturer in design, so has well-developed views of how their home should look, as well as the ability to make the one-off pieces that are in evidence all around the house. She is the chief executive of

Left: This quirky wall cabinet is part storage, part artwork, but looks great above a more traditional picture and retro bedside lamp.

a charity, and has a glamorous personal style and a clear idea of what she likes in the home. Their Victorian terraced house still has many period features, and inside it the couple have managed to create a subtle mix of styles that works very successfully. There are traditional pieces, a nod to mid-century modern, contemporary bathroom fittings and a range of styles of art; the house works because they have mixed these styles throughout and have kept to a very consistent colour palette, which helps to unify the look. Their home is beautiful, and they are both very happy with what they have achieved.

Left: This unusual sideboard made by the homeowner is a one-off piece that has a simple, modern feel.

Opposite: An alcove in the first-floor landing is the perfect place to add storage, and still leaves space for more of the couple's art.

What do you love?

Sometimes people's minds go blank when I ask this question, so I often start by asking them to walk round their house and tell me what items they love (or hate) so that I can start to build up a picture. While magazines and books are a great starting point, it is also helpful not to be restricted to pictures of interiors, since trying to find the image of your perfect home can feel overwhelming. Try to open your mind and think about your style in different ways; the way you like to dress, the car you like to drive, hotels you like to stay in or simply what in life inspires you.

CLOTHES The clothes you wear (or would like to wear) can be a source of inspiration. If you tend towards classic tweeds, you may like more traditional interiors; if you only ever wear neutrals, you probably won't want a riot of colour at home.

FILMS These are a great source of inspiration, because they often show an interior not only in surprising detail, but also in a lifestyle context. I started putting films with great interiors on my blog quite some time ago, thinking I would run out of ideas fairly quickly, but I have found lots of wonderful homes in films and am still finding more.

Left: I was inspired by a visit to Cuba a few years ago. Trinidad de Cuba on the south coast has the most beautiful Spanish-influenced colonial houses, and the interior styles I saw have remained in my mind ever since.

Below, left: These charming dressing-table accessories were part of the furnishings inherited with the owner's home. They fit the style of the house perfectly and evoke family memories.

Bottom: My grandmother had a book of photographs of her children, and sent it to my grandfather when he was away at war. Later she gave it to me, and I had it framed. Although it doesn't match the contemporary art I prefer, it embraces the traditional feel that I love and is important enough for me to want to have it on my wall anyway. I also use my grandmother's tea service, which reminds me of her and which I love.

HEIRLOOMS You may have inherited a piece of furniture or a picture that you love, but equally an heirloom could be the memory of a family member's or friend's style that you have always liked. It's generally not what people have given you (which may not be to your liking), it's what you have somewhere in your past that gives you a good feeling.

FURNITURE Finding furniture, lighting or specific products that you love can give you an insight into whether you prefer antique furniture, contemporary designs or a mix of vintage and new. Add pictures or brochures of products you like to your inspiration pile. It's also very useful to find pictures of pieces you love in the context of a room, to give you an idea of a particular mood and style as well as the furniture you like.

HOLIDAY DESTINATIONS It could be a favourite place or somewhere you have never actually visited, but something about it inspires you: city or country, seaside or mountains, Africa or Norway, Cuba or the Lake District – it could be anywhere. Look at travel brochures, travel sections in bookshops or online, or old holiday photographs to capture that far-away feeling, and you might find yourself drawn to a style that is specific to a country. I love the comfortable,

Left: My father introduced me to Sweetings restaurant in the City of London many years ago when we were both working in the area. Apart from serving delicious food, it has a style and ambience that I adore and would want to replicate at home.

Below: Browse your local bookshop for an interiors book that really inspires you – it will become an invaluable reference tool as you develop your own style.

Opposite: This arrangement of stones is a charming and individual accessory in an eclectic living room.

natural style of Scandinavia, so when I undertake this exercise, I tend to choose images of Sweden, which is a place I love to visit. You might find that the bright, breezy feel of a beach house in which you once stayed appeals to you, or you might be attracted to the warm, earthy colours of a Tuscan village in a travel magazine. Whatever it is, keep adding to your pile of images to help you find your personal style.

HOTELS Think about whether you would prefer a night in a swanky boutique hotel or a beachside bed-and-breakfast. Your choice of hotel can say a lot about your personal style, so if something appeals, try to work out what you particularly like about it. Make a note of any design features that stand out, such as lighting, textiles or overall colour schemes. Looking further into what you like about your environment will help you to know what you would and wouldn't like to replicate at home.

MAGAZINES AND BOOKS

Images of homes in magazines and books are a fantastic source of inspiration, and I use them all the time. There is an amazing range of both on the market. Find a favourite book or a handful of images from a magazine that you love and I guarantee that this will help you to identify or remind you of your own style. A few of my favourites are listed on pages 174–77, but you will have your own.

SHOPS AND RESTAURANTS

Your favourite retailers or eateries could also provide insight. Would you prefer to dine at a country restaurant or a newly opened sushi bar? Do you shop in designer stores (even if it's just window-shopping) or vintage boutiques? We tend to gravitate towards interiors that we find inspirational, and although you may not want to replicate them exactly, your preferences will be more revealing than you might realize.

STYLES If you already know a thing or two about the history of interiors, you may have a preference for a particular style. This could be anything from Regency to art deco, Baroque to colonial, Victorian to mid-century modern. You won't translate this style exactly into your home, but you should probably include a flavour of it in your wish list.

Appreciating other styles

Finding your own style will give you confidence and a clear sense of your personal design identity. You will be able not only to avoid pieces that do not fit in with your chosen look, but also simply to appreciate other people's homes, rather than instantly wondering whether you should have tried their look in your own. I adore what is often referred to as retro style (or mid-century modern), and when I see a great 1950s- or 1960s-influenced interior or piece of furniture in a shop, I am instantly drawn to it. However, I have long accepted that while others do this style very successfully, my personal style – and the look I feel happiest with – is very different. As a result, when I see something of that type I have the confidence to think, 'This is not the style for my home', and, rather than making the mistakes of the past and introducing changes that don't work with the rest of my home, I enjoy the piece in the shop and leave it at that. That is not to say that I don't have the odd retro item at home, but I wouldn't make an expensive purchase or have a statement piece (such as curtains or a sofa) in this style, since it just wouldn't work.

Understanding other people's styles helps to confirm your own, and allows you to enjoy beautiful interiors without worrying about how they compare to yours. Accept that all interiors are different and that all can be equally wonderful – just like their owners.

Having been very dictatorial about how to find your own style and stick to it, I am now going to give you a valuable piece of

This stylish living space is perfect for someone who loves monochrome, mixed textures and contemporary art. If that is not your style, admire it but don't copy it.

Mid-century modern style is a specific look: it is cool and makes a statement, and the design (and designer) of individual pieces is important.

advice that I give to all my clients: make sure your home doesn't look as though you've had an interior designer in. I am very serious about this. The best professional interior design reflects the style of the owners under the guidance of the (impeccable!) taste of the designer. The way to do this without the help of a designer is to implement your personal style in a consistent and considered manner.

Don't worry if a few of your decisions aren't strictly within the style. This doesn't mean that mistakes don't matter — they do, and the point of this book is to help you to avoid them — but a piece of furniture inherited from a beloved family member, a picture that holds great memories, or even just an odd piece that you truly love, will give your home the stamp of your character and an identity of its own, especially if the object is strictly speaking not your own style. Some of the hardest briefs I am given are when people buy a house or want a room designed and have nothing at all of their own to put in it. Once the interior design is done, I try to get my hands on a few of their meaningful personal possessions, to allow the home to take on the true style of the owner.

As your confidence in your own style develops, you will find that it will influence all the decisions you need to make to design your home, from selecting furniture, bathroom fittings and kitchen units to choosing accessories, garden plants and Christmas decorations. Understanding your own style will make all your decisions if not simple then at least manageable.

Left: The very traditional country style of this guest bedroom reflects the homeowner's taste and influenced the selection of new wallpaper and curtains.

Left, bottom: The fabric on this antique sofa is in a much stronger colour than is found elsewhere in the house, but — mixed with the other, very traditional, elements of the room, such as the romantic landscape painting — it provides a glorious and unexpected splash of colour.

The house

We haven't yet mentioned your home itself. That is because, while the architectural style is important, it should not be the deciding factor in your interior design. I am a great believer that a property takes on part of the character of its inhabitants, so if you start changing a house without understanding what you bring to the interior, the building's own design can overwhelm you. I am not suggesting that the period of the building is irrelevant, but interior design involves achieving a balance, and architecture is not the only factor.

Once you have worked through this chapter and have a good grasp of your own interiors style, you can turn your attention to the building itself. Of course, you may not yet own a home; you may be renting, living with parents or in the process of looking for a property to buy. If so, this is a very good time to identify your style so that you are ahead of the game when you do find your new home. If you have already bought your property, knowing something about it now becomes important.

It is helpful to understand the history of your home and what work has been done on it. If it is a period property, the way people lived at the time it was built will give you an idea as to why the rooms are laid out as they are, and why certain features were chosen. For example, many large Georgian houses have ornate skirting boards and cornicing in the formal reception rooms but basic skirting

and no cornicing in the original staff areas, and unifying the approach throughout the house helps to remove this divide – which does not (usually) exist in modern times – in a manner sympathetic to the house. If your house has been built recently, going back to the architect's plans or, better still, talking

The owners of this Victorian country house wanted a neutral, up-to-date style, and this look works very well with the period features of the building. Neutral walls and a classic stair runner in soft greens keep the staircase light and airy.

Teenagers have a wonderful knack of making their bedrooms their own, and it is a great way for them to start to find their own style. This young woman's bedroom looks absolutely charming — and I happen to know that it is all her own work. Fairy lights and a lava lamp (opposite) glow against the vibrant red and pink of the wall and chest of drawers.

to the architect or builder will help you understand why it was created in the way it was, what materials were used and any quirks of the plot or process.

If you are not sure about where to start with the fabric of your home and have identified your personal style, make a checklist to help draw out any key points you want to work with or to change. Consider what you feel to be the strengths and weaknesses of the property. For example, you might live in a Victorian terraced house full of interesting period details that you want to incorporate into the design, or you might live in a 1930s semi-detached house that lacks interesting architectural details but has lots of floor space and generous room sizes that you want to emphasize. There will be things you can't fundamentally alter, such as the fact that the house is overlooked, or advantages, such as beautiful views; these are worth noting so that you know what you are working with.

Once you have some insight into the property, and have made an honest assessment of what you like about it and want to bring out, and what you don't, the final task in this stage of the process is to look at how your style will work in the house. Living in a city where much of the housing stock is Victorian, I have seen some homes with beautiful interiors that are very true to the period, and, in contrast, some that have contemporary-style interiors. Both approaches are equally successful if the style is applied in

a considered manner. The key is to decide how much of the infrastructure it is desirable or sensible to change in order to incorporate your chosen style. After all, buildings develop over the years, so, unless you are living in a listed property or one of historical interest, you will be

able to update (or restore) it to a greater or lesser extent according to your taste. For example, if your style is very traditional you may want to install restored cast-iron radiators, but if your style is modern, state-of-the-art designer versions will be more to your liking.

The best design for a home happily pairs the architectural style of the property with the owner's personal style. The first steps are to understand your own tastes and — as a separate process — to appreciate the history (however long or short) of your home. Only when this has been done can you unite the two.

Warm colours and beautiful artwork keep this drawing room calm and inviting. Fireplaces are a focal point in any room, so their style is important. This one has a country feel, but is still elegant.

The living room is a winning combination of mid-century modern furnishings, contemporary art and a fabulous dark wall colour. On an antique table, sculpture and ceramics sit beside roses from the garden (opposite, right), and an antique clock (right) looks stunning against the richly coloured wall.

The owner of this wonderful converted Victorian schoolhouse is an art dealer and antiques expert. Her home is split between her living space and her art gallery, where since the 1980s she has specialized in selling contemporary art and sculpture. She has an extremely well-developed sense of her own style, and this is carried through in the accomplished work by the artists she represents, her exquisite home and her stylish wardrobe.

In her home, she successfully mixes antiques, mid-century modern furniture and contemporary art, and she is not afraid to combine expensive pieces with retail or charity-shop finds. Although her interiors style has changed over the years, she has retained many items of furniture and lighting from when she first set up home.

The gallery is an ever-changing feast as the owner holds different shows throughout the year. If you know your style well, you can happily mix old and new pieces, contemporary sculpture and antiques (opposite), or expensive art and a lamp from an interiors shop (right).

CASE STUDY
Natural tranquillity

The owners of this stylish city-centre home are a well-known writer and an engineer with a great talent for glass artistry. They are calm, considered people and have a large family, including a growing brood of grandchildren who visit regularly. Their home flows beautifully from room to room; natural tones and materials are found throughout, coupled with classic furnishings and many references to their travels.

Since they had moved house fairly recently, it was interesting to see that their style translated easily from a tall, modern town house to an open-plan detached house surrounded by a spacious garden and leafy views. Their furniture and art fit perfectly into their new home, and with the addition of bamboo flooring throughout the ground floor, neutral wool carpets on the upper floors and elegant, understated curtains, the house looks as though they have always lived there.

Furnishings have been kept simple and comfortable, and ornaments brought back from foreign travel and gifts from friends are displayed. This pendant light (bottom left) caught the eye of the household glass expert and now hangs where it can be admired from both the ground and first floors.

Opposite: These charming chairs (top) had been part of the furniture in a previous house but look at ease against the neutral wall colour and lined voile curtains of the owners' new home. The dining room (bottom) is light and airy, with glazed doors on to the garden.

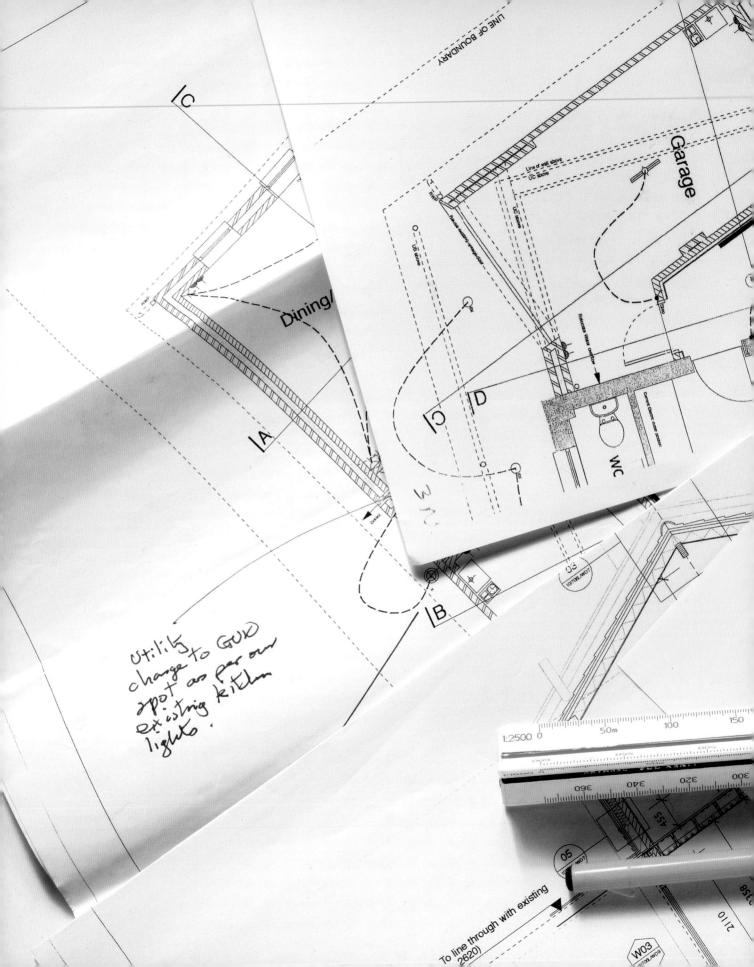

Study

SHELVES ABOVE (14)

400 BASE UNIT (10)

TRAY SPACE

PANTRY CUPBOARD (11)

SINK UNIT

(9)

DISHWASHER (15)

OPEN SHELVES ABOVE

500 UNIT

(8)

TALL CUPBOARD BUILT-IN MICHINE BROOM CUPBOARD (1)

BASE UNIT BASKETS+DRAWEL 600mm (3)

WALL UNIT 500mm (12)

OPEN BOOK SHELVES (7)

800 PAN DRAWERS 3 DRAWERS

(4)

Planning your home

The layout of your home involves more than just accommodating the various pieces of furniture. It needs to take into account all the activities of the household, and to provide the right storage, lighting, space and access. This is true whether you live in a mansion or a tiny flat; the principles of planning are about making a space function properly for the inhabitants.

If you are creatively inclined, the exercise of planning your home may initially seem a bit tedious, as it does not concern the way your

home looks but how it functions. You will probably be keen to get cracking with choosing colours, moving furniture in or getting building work under way. However, as with the exercise of identifying personal style, I go through the layout planning stage with all my clients, and I make myself do it for my own homes, too, as it is absolutely vital to the good design of a property and will help to avoid costly mistakes later.

The way you live

Make a list of the activities that are important to your household, in order to make your space work for all family members. If you can do this before you buy or even look for your home, so much the better. If you are planning a new layout for a home you already live in, put the rooms you currently have out of your mind and start with an honest list of the activities that make up how you really live.

Drawing up a plan

You will need to make a plan of the whole property in order to work out the best layout for your activities, even if you are concentrating on only one room, because you need to consider how you use all the space before deciding what a particular room should be for. The plan should be as accurate as possible and must include windows and doors; it is also helpful to mark the positions of radiators, electrical sockets, light switches, and so on.

Making the space work

Don't feel that just because the previous owners used a room in a particular way, or it was specified on the architect's drawings, you have to follow their lead. Try to think about what you need rather than the space you have. Extending or building from scratch gives you the perfect opportunity to design the exact layout for your requirements, but if you are not doing this, don't rule out altering the use of rooms, or even such minor remodelling as removing or adding walls.

How to produce a list of requirements

Your layout drawings will allow you to draw up a schedule of work that needs to be undertaken (from removing walls to putting in new electrical sockets) and a list of materials that need to be purchased (light fittings, furniture, radiators, etc.). The drawings will also allow you to work out where your current possessions could be accommodated, and even such details as where to place art and accessories.

Placing furniture

Once you've decided where the various activities are going to take place in your house, you will be able to think about what furniture you need. Do this without considering what you have already; instead, come to the perfect solution and then incorporate the furniture you own. Then look at how lighting and storage will work in each area, and also plan the plumbing for radiators and for kitchens and bathrooms if necessary.

The way you live

The first step is to write down what you need from your living space. This should not be a list of the rooms you have now or had before, but of the various activities your household would like to undertake at home. This will incorporate the things one might expect – sleeping, eating, storing clothes, watching television – and more individual ways of living, such as having an area for a group of friends to practise yoga, a room in which five children can do computer-based homework at the same time, or space for a 2-metre-long aquarium. These are all requirements that my clients have expressed to me, and that I have accommodated in my layout plans for them. However, please don't worry at this stage about whether you will have space for all the activities you want to allow for. It's possible that you won't, but unless you write them all down, you won't have anything to work with.

This space was originally a formal dining room, but the ingenious owner turned it into a games room with storage, which – with two teenage boys in residence – means it is used all the time.

The owners of this sleek home are great wine collectors, so a circular cellar with a spiral staircase was sunk into the floor of the kitchen.

This elegant hallway is the perfect space for the family piano, which not only looks beautiful but is also in a good space for practising.

Home activities

To help you check that you have covered everything, here is a selection of questions I ask my clients in order to find out what they need. I don't pretend that it is comprehensive – it is simply a starting point – but you will find that if you make a good first attempt with this list and then live with it, you will add to it as time goes on. For example, as your children come through the door in the evening and dump their games kit in the first available space, you can add 'place for putting sports kit, laundry basket for sports kit, washing/ drying sports kit'.

- How many people live in your home?

- How many people come to stay in your home; how long do they stay; and how many visit at the same time?

- Do you cook regularly?

- In which room do you like to eat?

- What sports do household members play?

- What hobbies do you all have?

- How many people in the household have or use a computer, and what do they use it for?

- Do you work from home?

- Is homework done at home?

- How much do you watch television? (Be honest!)

- Do different household members like to watch particular programmes? (Classic examples are sport and films.)

- How many people visit for supper/parties/coffee, and how often?

- Do you play games (chess/Scrabble/bridge/ poker/charades)?

- What about computer games?

- Do you read newspapers or books, and, if so, when?

- What possessions are important to you? (Books, art, clothes, collections, and so on.)

- Do you have or want to have pets?

- Does anyone in the household have any special needs of any kind?

- Do you have any staff that work with you or live in (for example housekeeper, nanny or au pair)?

- How much household admin do you do at home (for example paying bills, ordering supermarket deliveries, booking holidays)?

- Would you like to exercise at home?

- Do you regularly listen to music or the radio?

- Does anyone play musical instruments?

Drawing up a plan

Once you have made your list of activities, put it to one side, because the next thing you will need is a plan of your entire home. When I work on layouts with my clients, I like to look at the whole property, even if I am designing just one room. Each room works with the rest, and the only way you can see how a room could function is if you look at how all the spaces in the home are used. You need an accurate(ish) plan, ideally an architect's plan or surveyed scale drawing, showing all plumbing and electrical details. If you don't have a drawing and your project is large, it is worth commissioning one from a professional. However, the alternative is to draw it out yourself, and an estate agent's layout is a good starting point, although you will still need to measure up. This will take some time, but it will be worth it. If you want to draw it up on a computer, some very good free and easy-to-use drawing packages are available, but pen and paper are just as useful.

Most domestic buildings have already defined spaces – kitchens, bathrooms, bedrooms, and so on – and you will probably want to work within these structural confines. However, don't be too quick to limit yourself, as small structural changes, such as removing a wall or repositioning a doorway, can make an enormous difference without breaking the bank.

At the most extreme end of the scale, you may be building or converting your own home and have the ability to define your rooms. This provides huge potential and endless choice. Whether you are designing the space yourself or have employed an architect, it is very important that you create spaces that work for you, and the only way to make that happen is to define carefully what you need and insist that your needs are met.

Wall lights were strategically placed in this kitchen to ensure good light over the sink, hob and work surfaces.

This kitchen was small in comparison with the other parts of the house, so a wall was knocked down to incorporate the space into the dining room. Storage for crockery, glassware, cutlery and some food is near the main dining table but also convenient for the dishwasher. The kitchen works because a laundry and utility area (left) has been allocated off it, out of sight and general hearing.

Making the space work

Once you have your plan, you can begin to accommodate the activities and see how many you can fit in successfully. By doing this you will start to see not only what will work and what won't, but also what is really important and what could be doubled up or — if it is not important enough to compromise something else — even taken off the list altogether.

Start with the basics on your list: bedrooms, kitchen and bathroom. If you are moving into a property, these should be fairly straightforward, but if you are building or converting, they are the most important decisions you will make. Either way, these accommodate your big activities in life, and it is worth ensuring that they work very well indeed. Remember that you are just allocating rooms at this stage, so precisely where the bed, cooker or bath goes is not important just yet. If the estate agent's plan marks out 'study', 'dining

Below: This kitchen is extremely spacious and has lots of storage. An island unit provides a communal place for family and friends to eat.

Opposite: This modern storage unit in a teenager's bedroom is almost a work of art in itself.

room' or 'guest room', this does not have to be how you use the room; in fact, I delight in taking away all previous references to room uses and see if other layouts work. Very often they do, because everyone lives so differently.

The next step is to look at the individual spaces (normally, but not always, each room) and arrange furniture so that the activities are accommodated. Consider what is required for each activity, remembering that you can't be too precise with this exercise. Eating is a very basic example. Start by examining whether you want and would use a separate dining room, and whether that would be for most mealtimes or if you also want a less formal eating space somewhere else. Then ask yourself how many people would normally eat together each day, and how many on special occasions. This will help you to decide how large the table needs to be, whether it should be expandable, how many chairs you will need, and where all this should be placed in relation to the kitchen and your storage for plates, glasses and table linen. It can be tempting to think that, because you may have sixteen people for lunch on Christmas Day, your dining table has to be enormous. However, if the norm is eight including visitors, and four eating together daily, it would be far better to use a six—eight-person table with six chairs around it regularly, and have two chairs elsewhere in the house that can be easily moved; a lightweight foldaway table that can be covered in a linen cloth, and ordinary

chairs with Christmassy cushions, would do for the big day. Even if you have the space, it is not ideal for four people to sit at a table for sixteen looking at lots of empty chairs just because of Christmas Day lunch.

One activity that I find crops up regularly on the list is reading and the housing of the resulting collections of books. I work in a university town, and books are often a priority for my clients, so it is important to provide accessible, attractive bookcases and places to read. However, many people do not live in such a large property that a dedicated reading room is possible, so I am constantly trying to find spaces to double up as libraries. This may be a dining room, a spacious landing or a study that, once lined with well-made bookcases full of carefully ordered books, will look wonderful. However, because bookcases en masse can be quite imposing, I tend to avoid putting them in a bedroom, for example, where rest is most important.

The question of accommodating guests can also be overlooked at this early planning stage. Many people assume that a guest room is absolutely necessary, and that once it is allocated, the planning is complete. However, such an approach is likely to lead to wasted space and a missed opportunity of providing maximum comfort for your guests. The starting point is to work out how often and for how long visitors are going to stay with you. There is a huge difference between someone staying overnight and someone staying for a month, when space for clothes, bathroom use and storage of

suitcases need to be considered. If your guests tend to be short-term and sporadic, you may want to think about using your allocated guest room for other activities: as a dressing area, a space for reading or even a study (although if you choose the last option, you may want to consider a day bed or sofa bed, as I think working in a bedroom can be rather depressing).

The restrained use of colour and pattern, coupled with a favourite picture, give this bedroom a very inviting air of tranquillity.

In a large house, furnishing some of the guest bedrooms with twin beds ensures that the accommodation is flexible and practical.

FURNISHINGS

Planning the activity space will naturally lead you to your furniture requirements, and it is important at this stage to work not from what you have but from what would be right for your needs and your home. I am not suggesting that you throw out all your best-loved furniture, however; in later pages we will come to integrating the objects you own.

If you have allocated a seating space for relaxing and watching television, you will have identified the requirements for chairs and sofas based on the number of people you want to seat comfortably on a normal day; a coffee table or occasional tables for drinks, magazines and remote controls; perhaps a footstool that can act as additional seating or a comfortable chair in another room that can be brought in for visitors; and a rug to make the space comfortable and inviting. At this stage it is useful to think about storage: you might have a collection of DVDs or board games that you want to use in the space, or children whose toys will need to be put away in the evening. Also consider the

lighting you need: ambient light for entertaining and watching television; good task lighting for reading; perhaps even brighter overhead light for working, cleaning the room or playing board games.

Thinking through all the activities will help you to plan your layouts, and even considering small things will make your daily existence easier.

It may seem trivial to think about where you will unload the car after you have been food-shopping, and where you will place the shopping bags so that you can put purchases into cupboards and fridge most easily, but get these things wrong and they will annoy you every single time you come back from the shops.

USING CORNERS

One of the challenges of working with city-based clients is that space is often at a premium, even in expensive properties that at first seem very spacious. It is easy to miss areas that could be used to great effect and, if carefully designed, could enhance a room. Such elements may be simply decorative, to improve the look of a room, or also functional, such as fitting a desk into a living room or a library area into a landing. The advantage of working from a plan of the room is that once you have placed on it the main pieces of furniture, you can identify space that might otherwise be missed. Once you have spotted it, you can consider what use (either functional or decorative) can be made of it.

In a corner of a games room, a desk and storage space allow a busy mum to work from home.

MOVING BETWEEN SPACES

Once you have a pretty good idea of the layout of your main rooms, it is worth casting an eye over the way the rooms flow and identifying the main 'traffic routes' between and through them. Make sure that the main way to get from your hallway to your kitchen doesn't involve walking between your two sofas in the living room (or, worse, between the sofa and the television), or that the opportunity to reposition a door to maximize space in a room isn't missed at the planning stage, when it is easier to address. Going back to your list of activities will help with this. For example, imagine your guests entering your home, their view when they come in, where they hang their coats, which room you would like them to go into, how the cook in the house manages both to greet guests and to prepare food, and so on.

Similarly, it is worth considering the route of clothes from the laundry basket(s) to the washing machine, on to the drying area (outside and/or in), to the ironing board and back to the wardrobe, since you will follow it often; if it can be streamlined, life will be that little bit easier. American households often approach this activity in a better way: the washing machine isn't automatically put in the kitchen, and instead consideration is given to where best to do the laundry and ironing, and to the space needed for drying clothes

This generous landing in a country house was an inspired choice for an area in which to watch television comfortably.

This clever joinery under the stairs incorporates storage space for shoes and coats and smaller cupboards for glassware, music and other household items. Small sets of open shelves, painted inside to tone with the wall, provide dramatic focus.

and storing washing powder and other equipment.

LIGHTING AND STORAGE

When you have decided where your main items of furniture are to be positioned, look at where storage can be fitted in and also where changes need to be made to plumbing (moving radiators, changes within kitchens and bathrooms) and electrics (lighting, power sockets and network

points). It is helpful to mark on your plan all the lighting outlets, electrical sockets and switches that would best suit the space, and then cross-check with those you currently have. This will tell you what electrical work needs to be undertaken, and will form a basis of work for which your electrician can give you an estimated cost.

As regards storage, I try to work out what needs to be accommodated for each activity,

as I feel it can be a mistake to approach the matter simply in terms of what you own and where it could be stored. An example is in the kitchen, where storage is often at a premium: even if you adore cooking and do it every day, you will not need every single pot, pan, utensil and gadget permanently close at hand. You will need only those items that you use most regularly, and the additional items can be accessibly stored out of the way; that may

An ottoman provides a useful surface on which to place magazines or a tray of drinks, and additional seating when required.

be in the kitchen itself, but could also be in a utility room, garage or hall cupboard, or anywhere else convenient so that they can be accessed when required. It is silly to keep every single item of cooking paraphernalia in the kitchen, if you don't use them all regularly and space is limited. On a similar note, you may find it convenient to store plates, glasses and cutlery near the dining table for easy table-laying, but always ensure that the route to and from the dishwasher is extremely easy.

DO YOU REALLY NEED TO EXTEND?

I am often asked to look at spaces that have become problematic after an extension has been completed. A classic example is the town house in which a small kitchen has been converted into a large kitchen and living space, often incorporating an open-plan dining area and seating, with a sizeable extension into the garden. More often than not the extension is such a great success

that the family members spend much of their time in the new space, and the original reception rooms, once much-used, are now almost redundant, and at worst act as a corridor to the new room.

Of course there are ways to rework spaces for specific activities so that the rooms are given a new lease of life, but – having worked with some really good architects over the years – I have learned that the first question to ask my clients is precisely why they need to extend,

This little light-filled office
was created by dividing off
a section of an awkward
L-shaped living room.
A frosted-glass door allows
light into the hallway.

and what is lacking in the property as currently configured. Sometimes the answer is that the space is so badly organized and the storage so poor that extra space seems the only solution. If you are in this position, a thorough list of how you live and what you would like to achieve in the space will give your architect a good brief, and might even lead to alternative ideas so that you don't need to extend at all.

GATHERING INFORMATION

The final and crucial stage of this part of the process is to use the plan to draw up a list of work required and furnishings that you will need. Do this only when you are sure that you have identified as close to the perfect layout for you as possible. I normally tackle this list room by room, because it is simpler that way, but I then divide it into separate lists according to the type of work to be done (plumbing, electrics, decorating) and materials to be specified (flooring, light fittings, sofa, dining table). These lists will inevitably need amending as the project progresses, but the more detailed you can be at this stage, the easier to run and more cost-efficient the project will be.

This city flat is a show apartment for the smart home-technology company owned by a busy property developer. It has also been designed for his personal use, which includes regular entertaining. The main living area needed to include a cooking space, a desk, seating for watching television and entertaining, reasonable levels of storage and a dining table to seat six; and also to be a showcase for the high level of technology in the flat. A good flow between the kitchen, dining and seating areas was essential, and the television had to be visible from the desk area (something that had not been possible in the owner's previous flat).

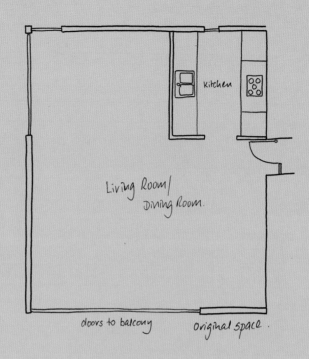

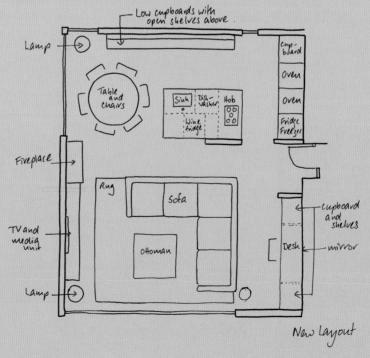

An island unit defines
the kitchen space while
allowing free circulation
through the entire living
space, and incorporates
the sink and hob.

A large L-shaped sofa and ottoman (far left) provide a comfortable space for watching television and flexible seating for entertaining. When planning your space, it is important to remember the accessories. The simple flower arrangement and charming sculpture by the television (left) look wonderful against the walls of midnight blue.

This specially built feature fireplace is visible from the front door and hallway. Each of its alcoves is illuminated with colour-changing lighting, and a gel fire in the bottom alcove adds an additional night-time feature.

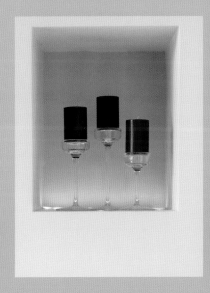

Family life

This traditional home was bought by a young family and needed updating, with consideration to be given to the layout and the requirements of a busy couple and their three young children. As the house was well over 100 years old and had originally been designed for a bachelor and his staff, there were some important changes to be made to the way in which it was used and the location of the main activities of the household.

The first important requirement was for a large family kitchen–diner with access to the sizeable garden. In addition, a playroom for the children was needed with space to watch television, do homework and play with friends.

One of the main reception rooms is now a music room and study. A desk for household work and working from home faces the fireplace, with storage on either side.

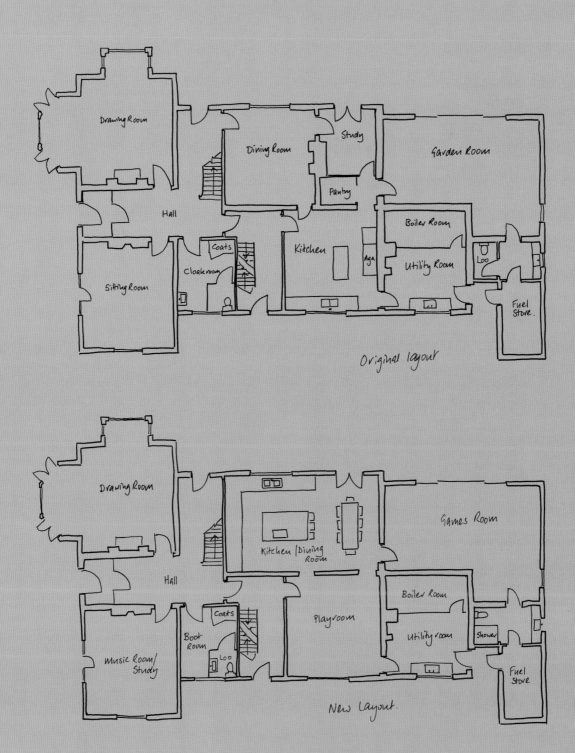

Drawing Room

Dining Room

Study

Garden Room

Pantry

Hall

Boiler Room

Coats

Cloakroom

Kitchen

Aga

Utility Room

Loo

Sitting Room

Fuel Store.

Original layout

Drawing Room

Games Room

Kitchen / Dining Room

Hall

Boiler Room

Coats

Playroom

Boot Room

Utility room

Shower

Loo

Music Room/ Study

Fuel Store

New Layout.

Right: Original features, such as these ornate doorhandles, were restored during the refurbishment of the house to ensure that the character of the property was retained.

Far right: The dining area was relocated to the enlarged kitchen, with glazed doors that lead to the terrace and garden.

Below: A modern, highly functional kitchen is at the heart of this busy family home, providing lots of storage and workspace, and also a sociable space for family and friends.

Left: The old kitchen is now a playroom with space for three children to watch television, play games, entertain friends and do homework.

Below: The main hallway is a natural divide between the busy kitchen and playroom and the quieter spaces of the drawing room and study/music room.

Also required was a place in which to work from home and undertake household admin, and for playing musical instruments, including a baby grand piano.

After much consideration, and investigating the options for the entire house, it was decided to move the kitchen and incorporate the main dining area into the kitchen space. A playroom was created off the kitchen with desk space and storage, and a formal reception room was earmarked for a desk and computer, book storage and the playing of musical instruments. The family have now lived there for several years, and the space works very well for them.

I hate my sofa!

I have more discussions than I would like with distressed clients about a long-awaited sofa that has been delivered and has disappointed in terms of size, style, colour or comfort. Sofas are not the only items with which this can happen, but I find that because they are a difficult thing to get right, the problem occurs more frequently. In any case, the way to address this problem is the same with any interiors-related mistake.

I always recommend starting from scratch, and thinking about the kind of seating that would actually work in the room, just as though the sofa nightmare had not occurred. I begin by listing the family's activities and the reasons why a sofa is required, then look for the best solution. As an interim measure, I consider how we can incorporate the sofa into the preferred solution. This is sometimes possible and sometimes not, but what is important when working out how to move forward is to put the mistake to one side. After all, if you bought a pair of trousers that you ended up not liking, you wouldn't go and buy a top to match; I hope you would buy a truly great top, thus ensuring that no one really noticed the trousers, and — in due course — take the trousers to the charity shop.

The owners of this beautiful home wanted to replace the sofa when they redesigned this room, so they ignored it. Now the room looks so elegant that the sofa blends in with the overall look.

Accommodating your children

Homes with children need a little additional planning, and kids' activities must be listed in great detail in the initial brief. Even if your home is small, there is no need to turn over every space to your children or — at the other extreme — to attempt to keep activities and possessions confined to their bedrooms. The requirements of every inhabitant are important and deserve consideration. Here are a few tips to follow when planning space involving children (either your own or those visiting, or both).

Below: This boot room off the main hallway is practical for storing coats, shoes and sports kit.

Opposite: Open storage of games and jigsaws in this family room ensures that they are easily accessible when needed.

❶ The best place for children of all ages to put on, take off and store shoes, coats, hats, gloves, school bags and sports kit is by the door that they most often use to enter and leave the home. Make sure you have really good storage in this area; if your hallway is small, find a place for storage as close as is sensible to the outside door, and kit it out well with hooks, shoe racks, durable flooring and even doors to hide it all away. It also makes sense for this area to be warm, to ensure that wet shoes and coats dry quickly, so consider fitting a small radiator or heater.

❷ Children, particularly younger ones, need plenty of storage around the home. They are not going to play in the living room and clear away their toys to their bedrooms when they have finished, so to avoid having to do this for them at the end of a long day, put some toy storage into communal living rooms.

Opposite, top: This lovely bedroom is charming for a youngster and will be easy to update when she gets older.

Opposite, bottom: Rules are made to be broken. This bed will not grow with the child, but while he is young, it is glorious and a pleasure for grown-ups to encounter.

❹ There is no point (and no joy) in setting up children's bedrooms so that they end up spending most of their time there. If you put a television and a computer in their room, that is where your children will be, not with you and where you can see what they are up to. Try to accommodate their entertainment requirements within the main living space of the house, where their friends can also visit, and try to keep their bedrooms for sleeping and the storing of clothes and some possessions.

❸ Children's requirements change over the years, so you will have to plan for their needs now and also in the immediate and mid-term future. This is true of all age groups, including teenagers soon to leave home, since they will probably return to stay for varying periods of time, often bringing with them lots of 'stuff' and, in due course, partners and even their own children.

Above: The painted knobs of this chest add a young and fun note to the room, and can easily be updated as its owner grows up.

Right: Children love to have space to play in their rooms, but they will want to have the option to play in other spaces, too, which is all part of the planning process.

5 Children's tastes for their rooms change pretty regularly and often without warning, so try to make your monetary investment in core, versatile items (such as a good bed, well-made wardrobes, a durable carpet and upgrades to lighting) and allow them a freer rein with accessories (cushions, lamps, rug, pictures and even paint). This will allow them to express themselves in their own space without compromising practicality and causing budgetary upset.

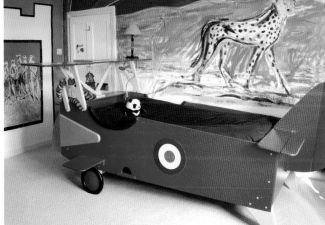

Choosing a colour palette

Colour is hugely important in the look of a house and contributes greatly to the outcome of a scheme. When I am working with a client, I like to establish their colour preferences early on, because this not only helps to reveal a person's overall interior style but also allows me to decide what fabric, furniture, flooring, pattern and texture they might be drawn to, which is vital when pulling the schemes together.

In this chapter we will look in detail at how to select paint colours. This is an area that many people, including professionals, have difficulty with, and there are some tried-and-tested approaches that I find very helpful when making colour choices. We will also look more generally at how to select all the colours for your home. If you can identify a palette of colours that you love, you will not only bring consistency and flow to the home but also gain the confidence to mix colours, choose flooring and furnishings, and include the right amount of colour for you.

Your favourite colours

This is more difficult to decide than most of us realize. When one is confronted with a paint chart or a book of fabrics it can seem impossible to choose which to pick, since the outcome could so easily be an expensive mistake. It is useful to start by going back to your original style choices from Chapter 1, but look also at clothing, current possessions or groups of paint colours to give you an idea of shades that you like or dislike.

Shades of neutral

If you are sure that you don't want much colour at all, and that neutrals are your thing, I'm afraid you still have lots of colour decisions to make. Neutral shades are fantastic but there are many of them, and you will still need to work out whether you prefer cool grey neutrals or warm creams, and also the extent to which you want to use such contrasting colours as brown, grey, taupe and black.

Colour combination

The colour in your home comes not just from wall-coverings but also from flooring, furniture, curtains, kitchen units, and so on. Therefore it is important to know what palettes and combinations of colour you like and how much contrast you want between colours in a scheme.

Style and colour

The style of a room or home does not dictate the colour scheme or how much colour can be used. Rather, you should find the right colour palette for you and then balance it with your style preferences.

Paint ranges

There are millions of paints on the market, and you do not need to look at them all to find the perfect one for you. I tend to work with two or three ranges of paint for each house I design, since I know that the colours will work well together. Narrowing down your selection to a few ranges that you really like will help to avoid confusion and mistakes.

Top tips

I can pass on a few colour tips and hints from my years of experience. Always use tester pots, but paint them on paper, not on the wall; look carefully at the colour in the room in question and at different times of the day; plan how the colours will flow from room to room, even if you are taking your time to work through the house; and, finally, feature walls can work very well, but try to have a good reason for them.

Using colour

It can be easy to think that the colour in your home comes mainly from the paint or wallpaper on the walls. These certainly play a significant part in the overall look, but it is important to remember that colour also comes from fabric in curtains and furnishings, flooring, rugs, lamps, cushions, bedding, accessories and artwork (among other things). As with identifying your style preferences, knowing your preferred colour palette early on will help to inform your purchasing decisions, as well as to pull your interior scheme together.

Unfortunately, there are no hard and fast rules about how much colour and pattern works, or how much contrast between colours will look good. This always comes down to personal preference, and you will know that you've got it right when you feel comfortable with the balance between the colours and furnishings in your room. However, sticking broadly to the colours you have identified as your favourites will automatically help to unify the look of your home, and this is why it is so important to define and use the right colours for you.

Strangely, the amount of colour a person is drawn to is not dictated by style; it's perfectly possible to have a colourful contemporary scheme or a neutral one, just as a country-loving homeowner may achieve his or her look with bold colours or a palette of neutrals. A colourful contemporary scheme may tend towards

There is a mix of blues, yellows, pinks, creams and dark wood in this bedroom, but all the colours are warm and similar in strength, for a tranquil, elegant feel.

In this colourful contemporary room, strong blocks of green on the wall and curtain are balanced with dark wood tones and patterned bedlinen to avoid a monochrome effect.

Pattern and colour are blended to perfection in this traditional bedroom. Warm blues and creams are coupled with fresh green, pink and dark wooden furniture.

Opposite: This tranquil, contemporary bedroom was designed to be neutral in colour; to keep it inviting, warm tones were chosen for the upholstery, flooring and furniture.

This country drawing room is a perfect balance of colourful curtains, chairs and rug with the rich tones of wood and warm neutral walls and sofa.

blocks of colour, bold graphics and possibly lots of colour contrasts: bold hues against white, daring stripes, strong geometric patterns or even a contemporary take on florals. A colourful country scheme, meanwhile, will probably incorporate traditional patterns and colours that blend (rather than being strongly contrasting), and feature colour throughout rather than as a burst of colour against a neutral background.

The lack of eye-catching colour in neutral schemes means that textures come to the fore, and this is often an area where

the style of the house will be emphasized. A contemporary scheme may have glossy surfaces, modern finishes and contrasts of black and white. It may also lean towards a greyer palette of colours, although this is not always the case. A neutral traditional scheme may include, for example, textures of linen, painted wood, plush carpets and soft lighting. Contrasts will be less evident

and the palette of colours may be warmer. Such small details amount to dramatic changes in the overall style of a home.

It is important, therefore, to think about the colours you love, rather than about which will create the effect you want. Fortunately you can have it all, so put aside your style preferences for a moment and concentrate on the colours you really like.

A modern bedroom and shower room in a Victorian house look fabulous in a neutral scheme. The tiny splashes of colour make a real impact.

CASE STUDY
Green rooms

I should hope that, as a result of thinking about your preferred colour palette, you will discover a love of quite a few colours, but concentrating on one for a moment will show how this can work. Suppose that you adore green. You have identified the style you like, but how will it work with this colour? Here are six very different rooms that feature green heavily.

A traditional gentleman's dressing room in rich green works perfectly with red furnishings, dark wooden furniture and gilt-framed pictures.

The textured green wallpaper in this music room and library blends with the bamboo flooring and off-white blinds and woodwork to create a fresh, classical look.

Left and below, left: This classic bathroom has rustic tiles in various shades of green in the shower, and the tongue-and-groove woodwork is painted a warm green to blend with them.

Below: Pale-green walls are the perfect background for a riot of deep pink in this pretty bedroom for a teenager.

Below: These Tongue in Cheek chairs by Peter Harvey are eye-catching in this modern living room (also pictured opposite), and echo the colours of the upholstery.

Left, top and bottom: This shower room features a lime-green vanity unit and mosaic tiles against neutrals to make a contemporary statement.

A large sofa in a strong apple green makes maximum impact against the subdued colours of the walls and curtains.

I hope this case study has shown that it is possible to achieve your own style using the colours (and level of colour) that please your eye. This gives lots of flexibility in choosing a look and colour palette. It is fairly rare that people like only one colour – although that can be the case and it is not wrong, of course – and most colours work very well if combined in the right way. It is helpful to find a range of colours that you like and use them in different proportions, depending on how much you like them and how strong they are.

Knowing what you like

This sounds very simple. In childhood we are often asked 'What is your favourite colour?', and we may have a ready answer, but as adults, when asked to choose a colour for walls or a rug, we often get overwhelmed. This is mainly because we tend to address the question only when we have to pick out a sofa, paint or flooring. As with finding out what style you like, it is important to consider your colour preferences *before* you are faced with choosing a product, and to step back and find out what it is that you really like, rather than what is available to purchase at the time.

Go back to your style notes
The images you collected for your work on your style preferences will help enormously with the question of colour, because it is likely that you will have unwittingly veered towards colours that you prefer. Lay out your style ideas, whether they are images, possessions or fabrics, and you will probably see a pattern. To show how this works, my project managers and I undertook this exercise in the studio.

In chapter 1, Jenny and her partner found a selection of tearsheets showing styles that she loved. It is obvious from these cuttings that they both gravitate towards neutrals (and most of the images they pulled out were of green/grey neutrals, rather than creams), and I suspect that for their woods they would prefer the mid-tones of oak and walnut over the lightness of beech or the dark tones of wenge. Overall they

My two project managers and I each selected several colours from our tearsheets as the basis of our own palettes, and the results were surprisingly varied.

Jenny's

Cate's pictures

Mixing the colours of checks and plaids can create a surprisingly elegant look. The most successful combinations are those that share the same basic hues, but in different proportions

FURNITURE Joseph Grange's desk, £1,680, Grange. Guilane bergère chair, £870 including pad plus 1 m of fabric, Clock House F... FABRIC Seat pad in Eriskay ER100... wool, 137 cm wide, £44 m, T... ACCESSORIES Mulberry tartan cu... Mulberry Home. Shetland throw in... Musket & Mazzullo. Adeli... Osborne & Little. Large shadow hide... Bridle in tray, £187·50; large leath... album, £99; pigskin deskpad... Fabric in background O... linen, 142 cm wide, £125...

Jenny's colours

Kate's pictures

Kate's colours

Cate's colours

This jolly chest of drawers
provides a charming splash
of colour in a traditional
family bathroom.

This is the scheme board I put
together for my bedroom
after a recent house-move.
I wanted a deep warm blue
for the walls (painted on to
the board), and accents of
lime-green, pink and brown.

confirmed that she likes warm, grown-up yellows and creams, and a palette that blends and isn't too strong.

I know from decorating houses for myself that I want lots of colour at home. I tend towards Prussian blue, lime green, warm brown and flashes of peony pink (in my wardrobe as well as my home), and I am naturally drawn towards pattern and mixes of colour; I also like quite strong paint colour. Although I love using red and yellow in my work, they are not for me at home. It's not that I don't like these colours — I love to see them in other people's houses — but I don't react to them in the same way as I do my favourites.

Others ways to find your colours
If you haven't got tearsheets or can't see an obvious pattern, look at the colour of your possessions. Whether pictures, photos, a sofa, a rug or clothes, it doesn't matter what you find, just that you like the colour. It is also important to select a few different items, because the object is not to pinpoint your favourite colour but rather to find a palette of colours that you want to use at home. Between twenty and thirty images and/or objects will start to give you a good idea; fewer than that and you might find that you are still stuck for inspiration. This exercise will also reveal colours that you are not so keen on: look at your collection of images or objects and think about the colours or shades that do not feature. This is just as useful to know.

have a fairly restrained approach to colour, and like their neutrals to be urban rather than country, even though their style is fairly traditional.

In the same chapter, Kate pulled together a range of favourite objects, showing that she prefers light, fresh colours that are warm in tone. She also likes a flash of china blue and doesn't mind a bit of red, although that would probably be used in an accent fabric or furnishing rather than in paint or flooring. She also had a range of tearsheets, which

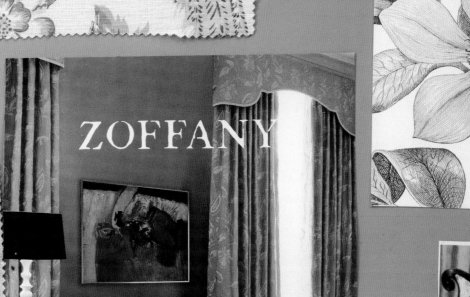

ZOFFANY

ANJOLIE

+44 (0)844 543 4764 | www.zoffany.com

Showroom Design Centre Chelsea Harbour, Lots Road, London SW10 0XE

Joa's neutrals

Traditional neutrals
These colours are a balance of grey, which makes them grown-up and modern, and green, which softens them, keeping the result warm. The swatches show (clockwise from top left) Slipper Satin, Lime White, Old White and Off-White.

Joa Studholme is a brilliant colourist and works as a colour consultant for the well-known international paint company Farrow & Ball. She once gave a talk to an evening class at my studio, and showed a captivated audience a great way of identifying colour preference. What amazed me was that she did it using only neutrals.

Joa groups neutral colours into four palettes, which are illustrated on the following pages. Each person tends to be drawn towards one or at most two of these groups.

Red-based neutrals
Soft, inviting and
warming, these colours
tend to be for people
who like reds and
yellows, rather than
blues and greens. The
colours shown below

left are (clockwise from
top) Joa's White, Archive,
Dimity and Pointing.

It became clear from Joa's talk that
most people in the audience knew fairly
quickly which group of colours they
preferred and also, significantly, which
were definitely not for them. Some
people liked two categories, but more
often it was only one that stood out.
As regards my project managers, Kate
knew straight away that she was in the
yellow-based neutrals category, and
she has already used Farrow & Ball's
colour String in her home. Jenny started
out by gravitating towards both the
contemporary and the traditional

Contemporary neutrals
The most sophisticated
colours of the range,
these work perfectly in
a modern home; used
with care, they are also
beautiful in a traditional
setting (below).

Pictured below left are
(clockwise from top)
Strong White, Elephant's
Breath, Skimming Stone
and Wimborne White.

neutrals, but has since opted for the
contemporary. I like the traditional
neutrals, and – although I generally
prefer stronger colours – I have used
the neutral palette for all my woodwork
at home.

Although this exercise employs
neutrals, and you may want more
colour, its importance is to help you
to learn not just what colours you like,
but also if the underlying hues of your
preferred palette are red, green, yellow
or grey. You will then know which range
of stronger colours to look at.

Alternatively, if you already know that you don't want much colour at all, this exercise will still be very useful. Strangely, if you like a very neutral palette, you have to work harder to make it a success, since there are so many shades available, not just in paint, but also in fabric, furniture and accessories. Choosing a colour palette will ensure that not only will you get all the light colours just right, but also, if you introduce any element of a contrasting darker shade, you will know whether to choose dark brown, strong grey or deep red, and so on.

The perfect paint

For the rest of this chapter I am going to concentrate on paint, for the simple reason that choosing paint colours, even when you know exactly what you like, is difficult. Wall colour forms such a large part of a room scheme that it is worth knowing some of the tricks of the trade. In the next chapter we will look at how to create your schemes (selecting fabric, furnishings, where to find key pieces, and so on), but, for now, let's talk about paint.

When working with clients or on a scheme for myself, I try to use colours from only one or sometimes two paint ranges, because the paints in a range have been pulled together as a collection by a design team, and will work cohesively together. You will still need to make your selection (even a small range can contain some 100 colours, and you will certainly

Identifying ranges of paint that you love will help you to find your perfect palette.

not need them all), but colours from a single collection are much more likely to form successful combinations than if you pick from many different ranges. Once I have an idea of a client's style and have seen the house or room in question, I will know which paint range will work for them, based on the amount of colour they like, if they tend towards reds, yellows or greys, and if the look is to be traditional or contemporary. You will find that when you have made good inroads into identifying your style preferences, you can start looking at paint ranges, and will be naturally drawn to one or another. I would then advise sticking to that range, although you may need to add colours from similar ranges if you find you are missing a particular hue.

I strongly recommend that you use a high-quality paint range. There is always debate within the professional decorating community about which brands of paint to buy based on quality and cost. I mainly buy paint from premium ranges (for myself as

well as my clients), because I think a paint with lots of good-quality pigment does look noticeably better when it is on the wall.

Tester pots

Once you have identified your preferred range of paint and selected some options from it, make sure that you buy tester pots. These are very small pots of paint that give you a sample of the colour; they are the key to avoiding costly mistakes later on. On a paint chart you are looking at very small patches of printed colour among masses of other colours, so it is hard to get a reliable idea of how the paint will look when it is on the wall. Don't use the tester pot to paint on the wall, however: take a piece of white paper and paint the whole sheet (don't leave a white border, as this can distort how you perceive the colour). When it has dried, pin it up on the wall. If it looks good at this stage, paint several more sheets in the same way and hang them in different parts of the room (particularly in areas of especially strong or weak natural light). Leave them there for a few days and look at them regularly, and you will come to know whether the colour is right for you. Also remember that a particular colour will look different in various rooms of the house; for example, what could look great in a north-facing front room might appear quite wrong in a south-facing garden room.

This restful drawing room is a retreat in a busy family home. Warm colours and beautiful artwork make it calm and elegant.

Colour and light

Any paint colour will seem significantly different in various lighting conditions, and it is worth looking at your sample shade in the morning, afternoon and late evening. The most dramatic difference will be between its appearance in daylight and in artificial light, and it is important to find out how paint colours will look under a new lighting scheme. If I am significantly changing a lighting scheme — and this usually involves adding more light to a room — I use a task light (a desk lamp or a floor-standing reading lamp) to see how the colour will appear under direct artifical light.

These photographs were taken in my studio, and the colours have not been altered digitally. We painted a wall in a glorious pale grey–green, fairly light but with warm undertones. We then took a picture with the camera in exactly the same place at 11 am and 3 pm, and in the early evening, and I was amazed by the difference in appearance. This is why it is important to live with any paint colour for a few days before decorating, and to look at it in the room for which it is intended, at different times of the day.

Colour throughout the house

Far left: Colour will change with the level and type of light, particularly in a long corridor with several rooms leading from it, so it is important to try colours out in the lightest and darkest areas before making your final decision.

Left: The dramatic dark grey—brown paint used on the walls and ceiling of this entrance lobby creates a dramatic contrast with the light walls of the hallway.

Just as with the style of a house, it is important to ensure that the paint colours you use flow well through the various rooms and corridors. This does not mean that they have to be similar or to match, but for harmony it is important that they do not jar with one another. Using a single range of paint throughout will help to avoid this. When undertaking a new paint scheme for an entire house, I like to decide on all the room colours before looking for connecting colours, for hallways, stairs and landings. Aim for a view from the hall or landing of a range of colours that happily combine, rather than clash, when the doors of the various rooms are left open.

Balancing the intensity of the paint colours used in this master bedroom and en-suite bathroom has created harmony between the two spaces.

Balancing colour and neutrals

If you find a colour that you love but feel it is too strong for the walls of a room, remember that there are other places the paint can be used for a hit of the colour you like without overpowering the rest of the scheme. For example, I like to use a stronger paint colour inside a glass-fronted cupboard or on the side of a roll-top bath; it not only limits the amount of colour but also draws attention to a good feature in the room. A trick that needs to be used judiciously but can be remarkably effective is to paint your walls a neutral colour and use a stronger shade on the woodwork. Soft greens and blues on woodwork against a cream wall will normally give a country feel, whereas black woodwork (which I have seen and greatly admired in homes in The Netherlands and Belgium) creates a wonderfully stylish urban look.

One final word on the use of colour relates to feature walls, where wallpaper or a particular colour of paint is used on just one wall. It is a good decorating tool,

This dark-grey wall is perfect in a contemporary-styled Victorian house. The artwork is predominately light, and the background colour creates a glorious backdrop.

In the same house, the attic bedroom is painted in light colours. A single wall of dark wallpaper creates a dressing-room feel to that area, and complements the light-coloured wooden furniture.

but is often employed in precisely the wrong way. A good feature wall draws attention to that particular wall of a room, perhaps because there is a collection of art that benefits from a strong colour behind it, drawing the eye to the paintings or photographs, or because you want to differentiate an area of the room. However, if your reason for painting or papering only one wall in a particular way is that you don't feel brave enough to do the whole room in that manner, you need to rethink your approach, as drawing attention to a wall that is no more special than the others will unbalance the room.

It was an inspired decision to paint the wall of this kitchen strong red and create a gallery of precious family photos. The back wall is mirrored for even greater impact.

Warm blue and cold red

This glamorous teenager's room is blessed with lots of natural light from two large windows. The combination of a cooler deep red and natural stone colours brings a sophistication that a warm red would not achieve.

There are many sayings surrounding the use of colour, and on the whole I think they are best ignored. If a colour or colour combination consistently looks good to you, then it is right for your home. Something I hear all the time is 'I can't use blue, it will look too cold', and this really is not true. The apparent warmth or coolness of a hue depends on the mix of colours that make it up. A blue that has red undertones will give a warm feel to a room, and a red with blue undertones will be cooler than a red with yellow undertones. For a warmer or cooler feel to a room, you need to select the right hues and then be aware of the combinations you are using. A green wall next to a rich oak floor, for example, will look warmer than the same green next to a grey slate floor. Generally, if your personal preference is for warmer or cooler colours, it is very likely that you will be naturally drawn towards those colours anyway, so forget the analysing (and the myths) and follow your instinct.

This useful boot room has been decorated in fresh white and warm blue for a clean, inviting look.

CASE STUDY
Colours of the country

This country house is more manor house than cottage, and has an elegance and grandeur that are enhanced with quiet, warm shades that come from wallpaper, fabrics and furniture as much as from paint. The owners wanted an inviting, homely feel for family life and a comfortable, well-presented house for their guests.

The palette is warm, with tones of golden yellow, apple green, cream, soft red and pale purple. Much of the colour comes from pattern – in wallpaper, rugs, fabrics or pictures – so there are few blocks of colour. A similar intensity of tone is used throughout the house, avoiding dramatic changes of hue and giving a calm, fluid feel.

Right: A warm, neutral cream colour throughout the hall, stairs and landing keeps the whole area light and avoids clashes with bedrooms and reception rooms, which are decorated in a range of colours and wallpapers.

Right, bottom: A charming toile wallpaper in warm creams and purples was used in a guest room with simple cream silk curtains and carpet.

Right: The dining room already contained beautiful antique furniture and pictures in warm brown tones, and a golden-yellow patterned wallpaper and simple striped silk curtains provided an elegant background.

Right, bottom: Not only do the family sporting trophies add a personal feel on the mantelpiece in the dining room, but also their colouring looks glorious against the wallpaper.

CASE STUDY
Up-to-date greys

This stylish, contemporary interior has been enhanced by the restrained use of warm greys and neutrals, providing a quiet backdrop to the dramatic furnishings. There is also a lot of black and white throughout the house, making a striking combination, and accents of colour are found in pictures, accessories and the occasional use of fabric, such as a window blind or a cushion.

Right: Black-and-white furniture keeps the dining room contemporary; the only colour comes from the picture and accessories.

Ceilings and woodwork are painted in the same colours as the walls, and where wallpaper is used, the ceiling and woodwork colour is selected to blend with the walls. This keeps the background simple, so that the eye is not distracted from the statement furnishings. Good lighting is crucial in this type of colour scheme, as the beauty of neutral colours can be lost in poor light.

Left: Warm wooden flooring ensures that this contemporary high-gloss black-and-white kitchen is still inviting.

Right: Textured grey wallpaper provides a great backdrop for a much-loved picture that would be lost against a neutral-coloured wall.

Below: The neutral tones of the family bathroom make the wooden bath the eye-catching feature of the room.

Below, right: The colours in this master bedroom are restricted to grey, silver, neutral and dark wood, with just a burst of brightness in the picture and blind.

BY ZIMMER + ROHDE

Creating your scheme

If you have worked through the first three chapters, you will now have a good idea of the overall style you would like to implement in your home, a detailed layout of all the various spaces, and some thoughts on the colours you like. Don't worry if you are still undecided about some elements, because it can take several iterations before one is happy with the results. We will now look at how to identify what to buy and how to visualize what it will all look like, and I will also give you some ideas on where to buy things. There is no need automatically to rush to the shops; some careful consideration first will

make the whole process not only easier but also more enjoyable, which it really should be, but sometimes isn't.

Make lists

From your layout plans, you will have a good idea of the work that needs to be done in your home (decorating, electrical work, building work, etc.) and also details of the furniture that is required, the number and types of lighting (floor lamps, reading lamps), and so on. This information is vital, and the more detailed you can make it, the more useful it will be.

Do things in the right order

At least make a stab at finding your own personal style, creating your layouts and looking at colours before embarking on your final schemes. It is almost impossible to create good, useful schemes if you don't work through these stages first.

Be organized in whatever way works for you

Pull your schemes together and present them in the manner that is most useful for you. There is no single right way of doing this; it is rather about envisaging the space and seeing what colours, fabrics and styles work best. I like to make up a board of style pictures, paint colours and fabrics. I personally don't find it helpful to include pictures of such products as lamps or furniture on the board, but I keep them to hand for reference.

Think beyond the usual shops

Retail shops are great places to find things for your home, but if you limit yourself to them you will quickly become frustrated with the lack of choice and individuality. Other sources to investigate include internet-based companies, trade suppliers, interiors shows, bespoke makers and second-hand dealers. To make up a really individual home, it helps to have furnishings from a variety of suppliers.

Understand the elements of your look

When you know your look, you may find that some elements of your schemes won't conform to the style, but that's fine. In my own home, I like a fairly traditional look, but I also enjoy contemporary art and need lots of really good lighting; I tend to stick to that combination, which works well for me.

Do your homework

The more you can research before buying items or visiting suppliers, the more productive you will be with your time. Order catalogues and samples before purchasing, check dimensions and finishes, and see if there are any local stockists of items you are interested in. When you visit shops, showrooms and suppliers, take your layout plans and swatches, and your list of requirements. The homework will all pay off, I promise.

Pulling it all together

To pull a scheme together, you must trust your own judgement. I want you to put aside any thoughts of what other people may think is 'stylish': this is about _your_ preferences. If you decide on a style that works for you, stick with it and buy only the things you really like, your home will be delightful because it will be thoughtfully done and will reflect your personality. This is what I try to achieve for my clients; my job is to interpret other people's requirements, style and colour preferences, and there is no point or joy in trying to force my own taste on to other people's homes.

The elements of your look
When I start to create my schemes, I go back to the style ideas my client and I have identified (whether through a collection of magazine pages, a book or other inspirational images or objects) and consider the components of that look. This will be a combination, but it is helpful to consider the individual products — furnishings, fabric, lighting, flooring or kitchen units, for example — as this will give you good ideas about how to translate the look into your own home, and will also help you to decide which parts of the look you like and which you would rather avoid. For example, I much prefer a classic look for my own home and I love antiques and traditional fabrics, but in art my preference is for contemporary; the images I tend to select for my inspiration pile often show rooms with

art that is more traditional than the style I would choose. That doesn't matter, however, as I now know that is the case, and I mentally block out the art in the pictures.

It is helpful at this stage to put aside the question of where you are going to buy the items you want and need. We will come to that in detail later in this chapter, but, for the moment, assume you can buy anything you desire. I know that you will be keen to pinpoint exactly which sofa you will be buying, in what size and at what price, but being too specific at this stage is a mistake, since we are still trying to build up an overall picture of the result.

You should by now have a mental (or an actual) list of the elements of home style that you like. You may have found that you like big modern leather sofas, or tweed-covered wing-back chairs; you may like floral chintz curtains, 1950s sideboards, Swedish painted kitchen tables or the clean lines of a white high-gloss minimalist kitchen. Hold on to these thoughts, because although you may not yet know exactly what your scheme will look like, you should have an idea of the types of things your completed home will contain.

Decisions to make
From your layout plans, you will be able to draw up comprehensive, detailed lists of the work that needs to be done to your home and the products you will need to select. Say you are undertaking a simple refurbishment in your living room, and you know that you are going to replace the

This elegant entrance lobby provides a welcoming ambience for guests and family, as well as useful storage using just the right furniture and accessories.

Creating this modern
bathroom from scratch allowed
the owners to specify the
layout, fittings, lighting, tiling
and storage exactly as they
required — even down to the
position of the television.

flooring, the lighting, the wall colours
and the furniture, add some storage and
reposition a radiator. You will need a list
of the required labour, which will include
electrical work, removing and replacing the
current flooring, decorating, joinery for
the storage and plumbing for the radiator,
and you will also need a list of items to
select: flooring, light fittings, paint, storage
design, radiator (if necessary), sofas,
chairs, occasional tables, rugs, a sideboard,
and so on. It is also helpful to have a list
of items that are staying in the room.

It is a good idea to start by creating
for each room a list of work and
materials. Once you have completed
this, combine the lists into labour for
the whole house and all the materials
required. Keep all the lists you make at
this stage, since they will most likely be
useful later. Also, try to be as specific as
you can: it will be more helpful later on
to know that you need one pendant light,
four wall lights and three table lamps,
than if you have simply written 'lighting'
on your materials list. These lists will
change (and probably grow), but they are
essential when sourcing the products you
need, and also when providing workmen
with a schedule of jobs to be undertaken.

*The layout of this bathroom
was carefully considered
before alterations were
made. Open storage was
incorporated both inside and
outside the shower area.*

Sample lists and materials

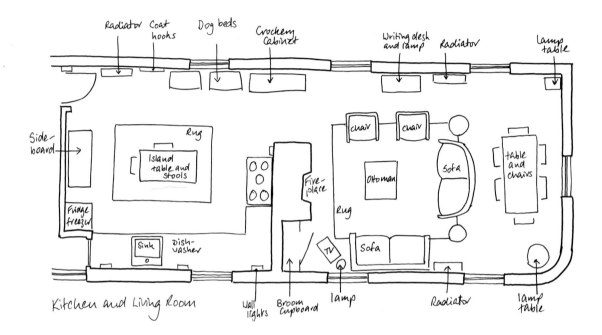

Radiator · Coat hooks · Dog beds · Crockery Cabinet · Writing desk and lamp · Radiator · Lamp table

Side-board · Rug · Island table and stools · chair · chair · sofa · table and chairs

Fridge freezer · Fire-place · Ottoman · Sofa · Rug

Sink · Dish-washer · TV · Sofa

Kitchen and Living Room · Wall lights · Broom Cupboard · lamp · Radiator · lamp table

I recently moved house, and as the building work was to be substantial, I had the opportunity to specify much of the work and materials. This is the overall list I drew up at the start of the project for the labour required and the materials I had to decide on and buy for my kitchen and living room.

LABOUR TO BE COMMISSIONED

Electrical work

Fittings to be provided, switches and
   sockets to be supplied

All current wiring to be stripped out, no making
   good, entire room to be plastered

Install four wall lights

Install one pendant light

Supply and install one extractor fan in kitchen

Supply and install fused spurs for range cooker
   and dishwasher

Supply and install ten low-level double sockets

Supply and install four high-level double sockets

Supply and install one CAT5 data point

Supply and install one TV point

Flooring

Fit and seal bamboo floor (flooring and
   sealer to be provided)

Adhesive – please supply

Skirtings to sit on top of flooring

Decorating

Supply and paint mist coat on plasterwork

Paint walls and ceiling in matt emulsion

Paint woodwork in eggshell – two doors, skirtings and window frames

Paint oil eggshell on exterior of kitchen units and plinths

Top coat paint only to be provided

Joinery work
(cupboard and skirting boards)

Supply and fit Torus skirtings, one curved corner

Make up and fit cupboard in living room including internal shelving

Fit kitchen cupboards

Fit worktop – one mitre and one shaped cut around the window

Fit kitchen door (will require cutting down)

Fit door furniture – two handles, one hook, one lock

Plumbing
(radiators and kitchen)

Plumb for and install three radiators (radiators and valves to be provided)

Install gas fire, mantelpiece and surround – installation only, chimney has been lined, gas connection in place

Curtain making

Make up and fit seven roman blinds, outside the recess. Lined and interlined, face fabric to be provided. Brass fittings. Cord and cleat mechanism

Tiling and hearth fitting

Oven splashback – tiles are 20 x 10 cm ceramic glazed tiles, four rows 900 mm wide, brick design

Please supply adhesive and white grout

Template and fit slate hearth, some levelling screed will be required

MATERIALS TO BE PURCHASED

Radiators – three floor-standing cast-iron radiators

Crockery cabinet – free-standing, antique piece

Island unit – free-standing table at worktop height

Two bar stools

Sink and taps – stainless steel, large bowl

Wall lights – four directional wall lights for above the worktop

Pendant light over island unit

Range cooker – 900 mm wide

Kitchen units – base units only, no wall units

Knobs for kitchen units

Worktop (no splashback)

Tiles for oven splashback

Rug for kitchen – to sit under island table

Gas fire and mantelpiece

Door furniture – door handle, hook and lock

Skirting and architraves

Two reclaimed doors

Paint – top coat only

Flooring including sealer

Fabric for blinds – kitchen and living room

CURRENT FURNISHINGS TO BE
INCORPORATED IF POSSIBLE

Coat hooks

Pictures

Sideboard

Lamps

Fridge freezer

Dishwasher

Shelves for above kitchen units

Two sofas and armchairs

Rug for living room

Two lamp tables

Ottoman

Television and television table

Dining table and chairs

Writing desk

Dog beds

Where to buy

Now you have your list of required items, and a good idea of the types of product that would be right for you, take time to consider where best to source them. It is very easy to rush out to the shops and see what you can find, but doing some research first will give you access to a much better selection and then narrow down your options before you even leave your house.

Magazines and books
I consider interiors magazines to be one of the best sources of information on good suppliers. There are lots on the market, and it will help you enormously if you identify a magazine featuring homes that you feel reflect the style to which you aspire. Some of the bestselling magazines are noted in the Resources section (pp. 174–88). You will find that they are all full of information on where the featured homeowners bought their possessions, with the suppliers' addresses normally listed in a special section at the back, and most also carry advertisements throughout and in a classified section at the back. This can be surprisingly useful if you are selective; remember that these are suppliers who have bought advertising space, so look closely at their website or catalogue and, better still, at the products themselves before purchasing. Getting the right magazine for your preferred style should give you access to the right kind of advertisements, since most advertisers select the magazine with the

appropriate audience for their product. I have found a very good range of suppliers over the years from magazines, and as long as you do the relevant vetting of companies and their products, this is a perfectly good way of sourcing materials.

Home design books can also be a good, if not as extensive, source of suppliers, as some include an address

This kitchen was dramatically updated when the current owners moved into the house. A central wall was removed to create a traditional, family-friendly kitchen and dining space that is now one of the most regularly used rooms in the home.

Wall units were kept to a minimum, with just a glazed cabinet, a plate rack and a bookcase — and the units were painted in charming deep green and blue.

book or directory section. If you find a book you love, some of those suppliers will be of great interest to you, and there is normally a very specific list.

Online
As is the case with every field these days, the internet is a fantastic source of information, but can be overwhelming if you search too widely. It is best to start

off at a recognized website, which will list suppliers that have in some way been selected so that you know at least that you are looking at a bona fide producer of interiors products. Although there are regular suppliers we use all the time, I am constantly looking for new products and often use interiors portal websites to locate them. My favourites are listed on p. 178, but there are many more out

Above: Kitchen storage does not have to be in wall units. This open metal shelving unit is practical and looks fantastic.

Opposite: This clever contemporary oven hood is a practical extractor and fits perfectly with the glossy black–and–white scheme in this kitchen.

there and they are, of course, changing all the time.

Once you have located a supplier online, I strongly recommend viewing the product in person if the supplier has a showroom. In any case, check to see what information you can get about the company, and particularly what its returns policy is should you choose to buy from it.

Trade suppliers

In your search for product suppliers, you may come across companies that say they are trade only. Don't be put off, however: although you won't be able to buy from them directly, you can buy from one of their retailers (most suppliers will tell you which is your nearest one). It is well worth finding these suppliers, which are often also the manufacturer of the ranges they offer, and going to see their product directly if you can. At least get hold of their brochure or product samples. The chances are that if you identify a supplier you like, you will find that it produces several items that you are interested in, although they may not all be on show in its suggested retailer's shop.

Retail shops

Although the general retail community is an excellent source of products, and I buy and suggest such products for my clients all the time, this is an area where things can go wrong. It is very easy to go to the shops and browse, hoping for inspiration, then get distracted from what you are

An attractive fireplace is a natural focus for any room, and comfortable sofas either side make this a very welcoming space. Delicate wall lights are the ideal style for the room, and give a warm light above the mantelpiece.

actually looking for, or see something that looks tempting but is not on your list of requirements. Also, unless (or even if) you love shopping, it is tiring, and after a day of trying out sofas you may just opt for the best of the lot, which may not turn out to be right at all when it is delivered.

The key to this kind of shopping, once again, is to do your homework. Take your list of what you are looking for; make a shortlist of shops that suit your style; take your room dimensions to ensure that the products will fit; and take other scheme swatches, such as paint colours or

fabric samples, so that you can check everything matches before you commit to any purchase.

Interiors shows

A great way to find suppliers is to go to one of the many home-design shows held throughout the year. These events normally last for a few days only, and the great advantage is that you can look at products from a vast range of different suppliers in very quick succession. The disadvantage is that they can be utterly overwhelming, as the items are even more out of context than they would be in a shop or showroom, so you have to use your imagination to envision the item in your own scheme and your own home. It is usually not possible to buy items at the shows, but you will come home with a good list of suppliers to follow up, not to mention plenty of inspiration.

The shows are sometimes open on different days to trade and general public, so plan your visit carefully. You will find a list of exhibitors on the show's website,

A matching wooden basin on a glass counter is practical and stylish, and the vanity unit beneath provides handy storage in this contemporary bathroom. An ultra-modern tap completes the look. Simple fixed glass panels create the shower area, and a useful inset tiled shelf is also an elegant feature.

100% Design

100percentdesign.co.uk

This huge show leans heavily towards contemporary design, and has many architectural products as well as interiors suppliers.

Decorex International

decorex.com

This show began as an exclusive exhibition for interior-design professionals, so it tends to attract high-end suppliers. It is very good for furnishings and other interiors products.

Formex

formex.se

This is the largest and most comprehensive show of Scandinavian interior design, and attracts visitors from all round the world.

Ideal Home Show

idealhomeshow.co.uk

This annual show has been going for more than 100 years, and is one of the best-known and widely advertised in the calendar. It covers many aspects of home improvement, including building, gardens and interiors. It makes a good day out even if you are not working on a particular project.

International Contemporary Furniture Fair

icff.com

As its name suggests, this fair has its roots in contemporary furniture, although the list of exhibitors is now very large and there is plenty more to see than just a fantastic array of contemporary design.

Maison et Objet

maison-objet.com

This comprehensive show features high-end home-furnishing products by both well-known and emerging designers from all over Europe. It has a very European feel.

and it is well worth browsing through these before you go to pick out those you want to see (and where they are in the venue); you won't be able to look in detail at every stand. A few of the best shows are listed in the box opposite.

Bespoke suppliers
It is easy to assume that you have to buy everything in finished form, but if you need an item to be a specific size, design or quality, it can be cost-effective to have it made. I often commission bespoke

joinery – sometimes fitted storage and sometimes freestanding furniture – but it is important to work with a good craftsman, because this type of design is a skill in itself. Commissioning a bespoke piece will mean that you can have exactly what you want, and if you choose the supplier carefully you will get a great product that will add value to your home and could become a valuable piece in the future.

Bespoke upholstery is another area that is worth considering. A good upholsterer will make you a high-quality

sofa, chair or footstool in exactly the size, fabric, design and interior filling that you want, and should also be able to give you all sorts of useful advice. Be clear about what you want and you will get a very personal piece.

Other trades that I commission when possible are stonework (such as worktops, hearths and mantels), flooring and rugs, plasterwork (cornicing and decorative details) and metalwork. I recently asked a local ironmonger to make up a row of kitchen hooks that was a great success and certainly cheaper than many less appropriate mainstream options.

Whatever you order from a bespoke supplier, remember to be very clear about what you are commissioning, as the piece will be personal to you and not a standard item. Ensure that you specify the size, finish, interior, colour and any fixings, and, very importantly, agree the price and specification and put it in writing before the work starts.

Second-hand pieces

I love incorporating second-hand items into my schemes, but for this sort of shopping it is necessary to be an opportunist, and to be very well prepared. You can, however, narrow down where to get your second-hand items, depending on your style and the sort of pieces you are trying to find. If your style is for traditional pieces, a good antiques shop is a must. Salvage yards are interesting places for anyone who likes eclectic interiors or an industrial style, and there are great retro and art deco finds to be had there, but I find it terribly easy to get carried away; stick firmly to your list or ponder a piece overnight rather than buying on impulse. Auction houses are another excellent source of second-hand pieces. It is imperative that you view well before the auction, but the adrenalin of bidding for and winning a fantastic item is worth all the effort.

Finally, do not rule out charity and thrift shops or online auctions. This way of shopping can be time-consuming, but the amount of money you save can be significant. And, of course, there is always the possibility of finding a real gem.

Left: This bespoke unit accommodates the owner's wardrobe and provides a clever place for the television.

Opposite: This dining room is a skilful blend of antique furniture collected from auctions and contemporary art and ceramics sourced directly from the artists.

Pulling your scheme together

Once you have found a few suppliers of interior products for your home, you can pull your ideas together. This will give you a clearer idea of what your finished home will look like. I find that the best way to start is by grouping the elements to see whether they work together. How you begin depends on the room. I like to start with the main elements that will make up the look of the space: usually fabrics and paint colours, or – for kitchens – units and worktop. For a bathroom, it might be tiles, paint colours, flooring and pictures of sanitaryware. The type of flooring is important at this stage, since flooring is a basic element of any room. Most suppliers of fabrics, flooring and other furnishings will send you a free sample, which, coupled with the sheets of

This calm and inviting master bedroom is made up of a combination of items sourced from antiques suppliers, shops, bespoke joiners, upholsterers and a local art gallery.

your proposed paint colours, will build up a good picture of the scheme and whether anything needs to be adjusted.

If a sample of fabric or flooring is presented in a book with lots of other samples, find out if you can order an individual piece of the particular material you are interested in, because the only way to test whether colours and patterns work together is to lay them all out without interference from other swatches. Many

The runners in these two very different houses are from the same company, but the looks created with paint, style of runner and type of staircase show that defining your style is more about what you choose and how you use it than where you get it.

fabric suppliers will let you order what is known as a returnable sample, which is a much larger piece of fabric (sometimes up to a metre) that will really help you to see how the final curtains or sofa will look.

Once you have laid out your samples you will know that you have got the combination right if the overall effect blends well. If it feels jarring or out of balance, try removing one item at a time or introducing others to alter the arrangement. If you are not sure, come back to it after a day or two with fresh eyes. Don't canvass too many opinions: you and your family are the only ones who have to like it, and if you discuss it with many other people you will get every possible opinion, which will just make you unsure and liable to water the scheme down to something bland.

When I am working on a scheme for a whole house, I like to go through this process for each room individually, because each should have a slightly different look (although there will of course be linking elements). Once you have completed all the room schemes, lay them out together to ensure that you have a coherent look for the property and to work on the connecting spaces of hall, stairs and landings.

The combination of a simple roman blind with an elegant trim, soft white woodwork and a beautiful window catch shows that attention to detail really does work wonders.

Presenting the schemes

Putting together some sort of board showing your final decisions for a room is a helpful reminder and allows you to look at your plans for the various rooms in combination. You can present your plans formally, with product information on the board, or simply, on a large sheet of paper with samples and images attached to it. I like to paint the board or paper with the wall colour for a room, and, if possible, I add one of my tearsheets to show the overall style I am trying to achieve. I attach swatches of fabric for curtains, upholstery and cushions, a sample of flooring (if possible) and images of any products I want to use. I make up a board for each room and sometimes an additional one for the whole property, showing the overall style and possibly also the colour palette (painted from tester pots).

Working file
Alongside the style boards I like to compile a working file of swatches and product information. This is not a project-management file of estimates, order notes, etc., but rather a design resource containing fabric cuttings, flooring samples, product information, style tearsheets, sheets painted in the colours I am thinking of using, and so on. It is easy to update, and I take it when I am shopping or visiting suppliers, so that all the information on my ideas is to hand when I need it. A file like this can also be useful as the project progresses, for checking details of products as they arrive or are installed, and also for checking that the correct colours and fabrics are being used.

The scheme boards for my own house were fairly informal because I was not presenting them to a client. I still made one for each room, however, showing paint colours, fabrics, flooring and inspirational pictures that reminded me of the overall style I was trying to achieve.

Living room

Kitchen

This scheme for a client's living room is presented on a board painted in the recommended wall colour and with fabrics and coordinating paint colours attached.

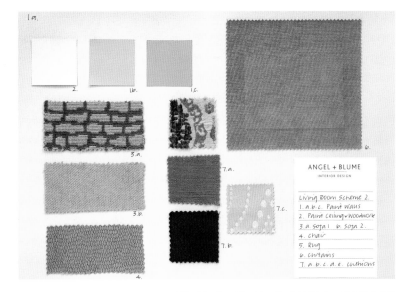

ANGEL + BLUME
INTERIOR DESIGN

Living Room Scheme 2.
1. a.b.c. Paint Walls
2. Paint Ceiling & Woodwork
3. a. Sofa 1 b. Sofa 2.
4. Chair
5. Rug
6. Curtains
7. a. b. c. d. e. Cushions

If many different fabrics are involved, it is best to note what each is intended for. It is easy to get confused, especially if you are working on lots of different rooms.

ANGEL + BLUME
INTERIOR DESIGN

1. Curtains
2. Bedthrow & lining
3. Sofa
4. Cushion 1
5. Cushion 2
6. Cushion 3
7. Cupboards
8. Cushion 4
9. Cushion 5
10. Cushion 6

I usually put product suggestions on a separate board so as not to muddle the scheme. This approach is particularly useful if a great deal of furniture is required for the room.

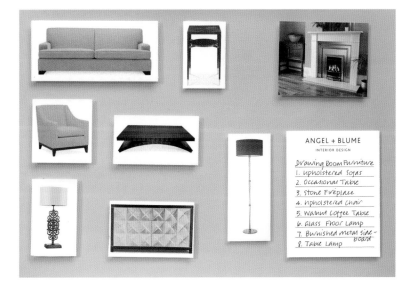

ANGEL + BLUME
INTERIOR DESIGN

Drawing Room Furniture
1. Upholstered Sofas
2. Occasional Table
3. Stone Fireplace
4. Upholstered Chair
5. Walnut Coffee Table
6. Glass Floor Lamp
7. Burnished Metal Side-board
8. Table Lamp

CASE STUDY
Bathing beauty

In this well-thought-out bathroom, a huge double basin overlooking the garden is a practical and attractive solution for a busy family.

This wonderful bathroom in a busy family home has been brilliantly planned and executed so that it works well for all family members and still looks elegant and inviting. The roll-top bath, painted a beautiful deep blue, is in the centre of the room, leaving the corners free to accommodate the shower, basin, lavatory and a full-size sofa (useful for Mum when the younger children are bathing). There is lots of storage, and the use of fabric in window blinds, cushions and a rug softens the look. The style is fairly traditional, reflecting that of the rest of the house, and neutral walls and a simple wooden floor stop the room from looking fussy.

The eaves are used to best advantage by incorporating a made-to-measure shower enclosure. Beautiful natural slate tiles are a hard-wearing and stylish finish in this corner.

CASE STUDY
On home territory

While I was writing this book, I was also overseeing a building project of my own – so I tried to follow my own advice! As I had to strip out the interior of the property, I had a blank canvas for the layout, which I planned in great detail, mainly because the space is small and I had lots to fit in. Before I started, I knew the style I wanted (more traditional than in my last house), the colour palette and also most of the fixtures and fittings.

I faithfully followed my own schemes and product selections

Although the kitchen and living area in my home are essentially one open space, there is a half wall that provides a natural division. I therefore created a different scheme for each area, but ensured a visual flow by using harmonizing colours and fabrics and running the flooring throughout the space.

until it came to the decorating, when I suddenly decided to paint the bathroom green rather than the more neutral colour I had originally chosen. It might have worked if I had had a good reason for it, but I didn't; it looked truly awful and I had it redecorated immediately in the colour I had first picked out. So, take it from me, it is worth following the schemes you have created, unless you have a very good reason for deviating from them.

Above: The bathroom has less natural light than the other rooms in my house, so a softer, lighter wall colour worked best. I opted for traditional fittings, including a roll-top bath and a classic black–and–white checked floor.

Left: I bought my bed in an antiques shop many years ago, and it has featured in the last three houses I have owned. For this new home, I knew I wanted a fairly strong, deep blue for the walls, and my old curtains work reasonably well while I wait for the new ones to be made up.

INVOICES

CORRESPONDENCE

ESTIMATES

Rhapsody in colour

marmoleum® global 3

LINOLEUM

Managing your project

Tight coordination of your project, whether it involves extensive building work or just a revamp of your soft furnishings, is absolutely vital, not just to keep control of your budget and timetable but also to ensure that the design schemes you have worked so hard on are implemented in the way you envisaged, and with the right level of quality and finish. A well-managed project will also be more enjoyable, or at least less stressful, and you will get on better with your contractors, workmen and suppliers.

Write detailed specifications

This sounds very involved, but for most interiors projects it simply amounts to a thorough, well-thought-out list giving as much detail as possible about what needs to be done. For a big building project, drawing up these specifications will be more complicated, and you will probably need the help of an architect or an architectural technician.

Little things that make all the difference

Before any work begins, think about which WC the visiting workmen should use; where they can make a cup of tea; how you can get hold of them and they of you; who will oversee deliveries; where rubbish will go; and whether your neighbours need to be informed of noisy or disruptive work.

Who will manage the project?

The old saying goes that the role of project manager involves finishing the project on time, on budget and to the brief. Although these three are achievable in any size of project, it is rare for problems not to arise along the way, so what you need is someone who can calmly address the problems – whether they arise from the building, the workforce, the supplier or the design itself – and keep the project on track.

Find good tradesmen

This is one of the hardest parts of a project, and there is no easy way to do it. Start with a recommendation from someone who has used a workman recently. Ask for and follow up references; ask them to do a small piece of work first if possible; and check that all contractors have the relevant insurance by asking for a copy of their policy.

Why you need a project manager

Whatever your project, someone needs to manage the day-to-day running of the work, and it is vital to establish who is doing this and the scope of the responsibility. The role may fall to an external project manager, the building contractor, the architect, the interior designer or you; the important thing is that both you and the person undertaking the role know that the responsibility is with them.

Work to be done

It may sound obvious, but the first task is to write a really good list of what needs to be done. I first note everything room by room (and this process may have begun as part of the layout plans in the design work). I include as much detail as possible and record everything, large or small, even if items on the list are likely to become relevant only at a later date. I also add notes for myself of things that may be useful to think about when planning the project: items of furniture that are to be retained, if a carpet is to be kept (handy for the workmen to know), if pictures are to be rehung on current hooks so the fixings need to stay in the wall, if a piano will need to be moved (which may be a specialist job), and so on. If possible, do this by going into each room with the plan to hand. That way you will notice small things needing to be addressed that are not obvious from the plan.

Once you have as thorough a list as possible, re-order the entries into materials to be bought or ordered and work that needs to be undertaken. Unless you are commissioning one contractor to do all the work, you should group the work by trade: builder, plumber, electrician, plasterer, decorator, tiler, floorer, joiner, curtain fitter, and so on. These lists will form the basis of the tradesmen's estimates and the checklist you will need as the project progresses. I like to attach the details of the relevant materials to the list of work so that there are no surprises for the tradesmen when the work starts. For example, the

plumber may take only an hour to plumb in a very simple washbasin that he is familiar with, but if he is to fit something more elaborate, he will need to know before estimating the cost and certainly before starting the work. Your lists should also specify practical requirements about getting rid of anything you don't need: such requests as 'remove old bathroom fittings from site', 'take up and remove old carpet' or 'remove current kitchen but retain units for use in utility room'.

Opposite: This desk and storage were made by a local joiner to fit the space. A bespoke mirror was added to the back of the desk so that anyone sitting there can see the television without having to turn around.

Above: Lighting concealed behind these shelves is invisible during the day but creates a dramatic effect at night.

151

Meeting a deadline

The owners of this spacious new-build home had a specific timetable for the interior work. The house incorporates a home office and media room from which one of the family members runs a busy company, and planning the project well was vital to keep the business running smoothly.

A comprehensive scope of work was put together, including detailed joinery drawings, enabling timings and costs to be provided by the relevant contractors. A provisional timetable was then drawn up, dependent on the developer completing its work, and supplied along with the scope of work to all the parties involved. Adjustments were made as required and the project was tightly managed after the start of the work, including the coordination of the household move, which involved children, a dog, a business and many, many boxes.

A television at the appropriate height for comfortable viewing is essential in a media room. Large cupboards keep this room free from clutter, and decorative alcoves are discreetly lit to highlight favourite accessories.

Finding good tradesmen

Finding good workmen is difficult, but it is crucial to the success of a project, and to preserving your own sanity. One of the best ways is to get a recommendation from someone who has had work done recently. If you are given the details of a tradesman who is a friend or a family member, however, and your contact hasn't worked with them (or even sometimes if they have), avoid following it up, as it can lead to upset.

Once you have a good recommendation, meet the person and see if you like them. This sounds rather superficial, but it is important that you get on because you will have a lot to do with each other during the course of the project, and should things get difficult (which they often do) you need to feel that you will be able to resolve matters amicably. It is also important, if the work is of any significant extent, to get references from satisfied customers and view the work they had done. Don't be embarrassed to ask for this, as anyone with a decent work history will be only too happy to let previous customers sing their praises. If they can't produce names of happy customers, or don't seem keen, there is a problem.

If you are able to, ask the contractor to undertake a small amount of work for you first. I try to get tradesmen I have not used before to do something for me in my own home before I ask them to undertake work at a client's house, so that I can check the quality of their work, that they leave the home tidy, that they turn up on time and that they stick to their estimates.

Left: As part of the refurbishment of this family home, an attractive fireplace was retained and minor repairs carried out to improve its appearance.

Left, bottom: This family bathroom was created by knocking a shower room and cloakroom together. To minimize disruption to the household, a very tight schedule was worked out and materials were purchased beforehand and stored on site.

Finally, ask for a copy of their insurance policy. A contractor carrying out work in someone else's home should have insurance so that if they damage anything, it can be claimed for. Accidents do happen, and it is an unhappy situation all round if the matter can't be settled properly.

Coordinating the work

The homeowners' existing furniture fitted the bay window of their new drawing room perfectly. The floor was stripped and polished, the walls and woodwork were painted and new curtains were hung to give a new lease of life to a tired room.

However large or small your project, it is important that you establish who is managing it. The role may be allocated to an independent project manager specially employed by you; to the building contractor as part of the overall brief; to someone else, such as an architect or interior designer; or to you. If you don't establish formally who is taking on the management role, your project will almost certainly be shambolic, and one or more parties will feel aggrieved during the course of the work.

If your project is fairly large, and certainly if you are extending significantly or building from scratch, you will probably be working with an architect. If so, don't assume that they will manage all the day-to-day details of the work; it may be that this is the case, but you will need to check.

The role of project manager is to make sure the various contractors are brought in at the appropriate time to undertake work that has been correctly specified. It involves drawing up a sensible, realistic timetable, then managing and communicating to you any alterations that need to be made along the way; implementing the design specified by you, the architect or the interior designer; and producing and sticking to an estimate of the cost for the whole project (or communicating changes to you) according to the specifications provided.

Using a project manager

If you are using a dedicated project manager, either as part of the architectural or interior-design work or as supplied by your building contractor, the role still needs to be defined clearly. This person will be paid for by you, whether it is estimated separately or as part of the overall building or architectural contract, so get the most from it and undertake your part of the work properly, as this will help to achieve a good outcome.

A project manager should provide you with a schedule, well presented so that you can understand it and with enough detail that you know when things are going to occur and when you will be needed for meetings, to make decisions or to review

This bathroom was fitted into the eaves. It involved building new internal walls, altering plumbing and electricity, and fitting the bathroom. One element of the organization was getting materials, tools and building rubbish up and down three flights of stairs.

This stunning pendant light above the main staircase was tricky to fit; not only was the spot hard to reach, but also the fitting needed to be assembled by putting each flower in place.

This double-height living room with a mezzanine is stuffed full of beautiful antiques and artwork and an ornate chandelier — all of them things to be considered when redecorating.

progress. It will help you to plan your life: when you need to remove possessions from a room, hand over keys or let tradesmen into the property; when you need to move out; and when you can move back in.

You should also agree in writing to a detailed estimate of the cost of the work before the project commences, and your project manager should monitor it throughout. Any additional cost should be agreed with you before it is incurred, and a satisfactory explanation supplied.

Your project manager will also be responsible for such aspects as the security of your home if you are handing over a set of keys, or, if you are letting people in each morning, informing you who will be arriving and when. He or she will coordinate deliveries of materials and the removal of rubbish from the site (including packaging), and will arrange to let your neighbours know about disruptive work or effects on communal parking.

CASE STUDY
Faded Grandeur

This lovely farmhouse had a charming feel to it already but was in desperate need of a complete update, so it was important to the owners not only to make the space express their own style but also to retain a sense of the property's history. A programme was undertaken to redecorate, replace bathrooms, change flooring and make small structural changes. New soft furnishings, light fittings and furniture were carefully selected to sit comfortably with the family's heritage pieces.

In order to manage the project, a detailed scope of work was drawn up for each room, and this was then divided by trade. Specifications for each piece of work were provided with as much detail as possible. For example, the decorating schedule noted colours for walls, ceilings and woodwork, whether picture hooks and curtain rails should be removed, and if door and window furniture was to be replaced or retained. A timetable was drawn up and given to every contractor involved. Even after such detailed preparation, a project manager visited the site every day that work was taking place, to answer questions or tackle problems that arose.

Opposite, top: Fresh paint, flooring, curtains and bespoke fitted bookshelves provided a refreshed backdrop to the family's furnishings and artwork.

Opposite, bottom: The family bathroom was in desperate need of updating, but it was important that the new look blended comfortably with the rest of the house.

Below, left: The dining-room bookcase was retained, as it provides useful storage. New wallpaper, curtains and light fittings considerably updated the room.

Below, right: The wallpaper and curtains for this charming guest bedroom were selected carefully to reflect the style of the rest of the house, and to make the room look as though it had always been that way.

Far left: A stack of the family's china is the perfect accessory.

Centre: Fresh new wallpaper in a traditional pattern has brightened the family dining room.

Left: New door furniture was added throughout, but in a traditional style in keeping with the look of the house.

Being your own project manager

If you choose to manage your project yourself, you will make considerable cost savings, and you will be in charge of the outcome, ensuring that it is exactly as you had envisaged. However, be prepared for it to be more work than you bargained for. If you have no training or experience in project management, you may still be very able, since I find that the best project managers have lots of common sense, an ability to talk to anyone and the capacity to stay calm in a crisis. The rest can be learned.

Getting estimates
Once you have a specification of work (this is the list from your layout planning and work on the design scheme), get quotations from the relevant workmen. If you already know of a contractor you like and trust, you probably need to get only one estimate, but if you are in any doubt, get two or three. Any more is a waste of your time and theirs, so try to get some credible candidates at the outset.

Once you have an estimate that you are happy with in terms of both the price and the amount of detail, make sure that you accept the estimate in writing and, at the same time, note that any extras should be communicated to and agreed with you before the cost is incurred. Extras are so often the source of upset that putting this in writing not only protects you but also puts the subject clearly into the mind of the person providing the estimate.

Whatever the size of your project, it is prudent to have a contingency fund to cover additional items that crop up as it goes along. This is to pay for any element that could not have been anticipated or that has been forgotten in the specification; these things can and do occur, even in the most tightly managed project. As a minimum, I would suggest a contingency fund of 10% of the overall cost of the project, and for larger building works I would put aside a 20–30% contingency. This is simply a notional figure for you to take into consideration, but you must know that you can find it should the need arise. Such financial breathing space will allow you to sleep

An unattractive mantelpiece was removed from this living room and a simple space created for the woodburner.

This bookcase was made by a local joiner to the specification of the homeowner.

the more information you can include the better. You will get many comments as you send it round, as every trade has a view on the best order for the jobs and the way they should be organized. Some will be invaluable and some should be ignored, but all should be considered. Once the timetable is agreed, it will become one of your most useful documents and should be reviewed every day of the project.

Paperwork
A crucial aspect of project management is keeping your paperwork in order and accessible. If you are a naturally organized person, this won't be a huge chore, but if, like me, you err on the side of ordered chaos, it is worth forcing yourself to do it (or getting someone to help you with it). By paperwork I mean specifications of work, drawings, estimates and invoices from workmen, product information, useful contact details, and any formal documentation, such as planning permission or building-control documents and insurance certificates. You will need all this information to hand as the project progresses, and if you can find it quickly you will save time, money and aggravation.

You will work out your own way to file your project paperwork, but the one thing I would highly recommend is the 'working' file that you take to all your meetings. It is amazing how often this sort of information can solve an

This airy hallway connects with the kitchen, dining area and family room beyond, using the same limestone flooring and paint colours. The stairs were painted deep grey, and an eye-catching runner in strong purple and pink creates a comfortable surface.

more easily during the course of the project; if it is not required, think of it as a well-earned bonus for a carefully managed project.

Timetable
A good timetable will help all concerned, but particularly you in your role as project manager. It is drawn up by establishing the amount of time each tradesman thinks he will need for each item on the specification of works, and listing jobs in order. You will then need to factor in the lead times of the materials involved and also incorporate any dates that are essential to you. As with the budget, incorporate a contingency (a minimum of one or two days per trade) for unavoidable delays. This breathing space will avoid you having to reorganize each time something unforeseen occurs.

Circulate the timetable in writing to everyone involved. It does not matter how it is presented, but, as a rule of thumb,

This spacious room could have felt too large for its young occupant, but warm colours and pretty accessories keep it inviting and cosy.

immediate problem, and it also provides you with a sense of organization and calm that is useful in the middle of a project.

Snagging

At the end of every project, however large or small, there is the chance to examine the work and point out small errors or omissions. Any tradesman will be expected to put these right within the scope of the work agreed and to proper standards of workmanship, and while this does not mean that you can demand any changes that seem right to you, it does allow you to inspect the work and agree one round of corrections to be undertaken without further cost to you. Large problems should be raised as they occur, but smaller things, such as marks on the paintwork, the clearing up of inoffensive rubbish, or anything that seems simple to rectify, are best noted down, agreed with each tradesman and then undertaken in one last round of work at the end of the project.

Little things that make all the difference

I have found that there are a few very small things that make all the difference to goodwill during a project. Here are my top tips:

Tea and coffee

It may seem friendly to offer tea and coffee to the first arrivers on the first day (and don't be afraid to do this – it sends out a good message), but are you happy to make it several times a day, every day, during the course of the project? Agree the arrangements for this at the very beginning, and remember that it is perfectly acceptable to expect the tradesmen to make it themselves. In fact, many bring their own kettle and mugs, but a place to put them and milk in the fridge will be appreciated.

Cloakroom

If contractors are with you all day, they will need to use the WC, so show them to one you are happy for them to use.

Your phone number

During the day-to-day project work, questions will arise that only you, as project manager, can answer, and although you may think absolutely everybody has your phone number, it is not worth taking the risk. Place your phone numbers (or any alternative contact information) somewhere really obvious. I normally write it on as many walls as I can find, but these may get knocked down, plastered or decorated, so think about the best system for your project.

Plans and specifications

Plans and specifications should be in the hands of all your workmen, too, but my advice is to assume that they don't have them and to keep a set on site, preferably taped to the wall for all to see. Then there is no excuse for instructions not to be followed to the letter.

Materials

Most refurbishment work requires some new materials, and these items will need to be delivered to your home and to be ready for the workmen when they need them. It is important that materials are on site before the start of the project so that workmen know what they are installing, and so that any questions or problems relating to the product can be addressed early on. Part of the project manager's role is to know when materials will be delivered

This area in a hallway accommodates the family's piano, and the wood-burning stove makes it a pleasant place for practice.

and, crucially, where they are to be stored while the work is under way. For example, if your project is to refurbish a bathroom, you will need all the sanitaryware on site almost at the start of the project so that the plumbers know what pipework needs to be provided for your selected basin, bath, WC, shower, and so on. They will not actually install the items until the flooring, decorating, joinery and tiling have been done, however, so you need to work out where the sanitaryware will live until it is needed.

Protection of work

Although it is every tradesman's duty to treat your home with care so that no damage is done, there are some things you can do, or request to be done, that will greatly help to ensure that accidents don't happen. For example, if you are having an en-suite bathroom refurbished, you may want to have a carpet fitter take up the bedroom carpet and re-fit it once the work is completed. Alternatively, you could request that the tradesmen involved cover the entire room in dust sheets as part of the specification of works.

Thinking about what a tradesman will need in order

A welcoming hallway is important in every home, for both residents and guests. Try not to clutter it with coats and shoes, but use the space for a lamp table and a place on which to put flowers, keys and post.

An elegant upholstered bedhead, valance and bedcover look fabulous in this stylish master bedroom.

to undertake the work will also help to avoid upset. A joiner will need an outside space in which to cut wood; this will inevitably produce wood shavings and dust, so offer a space that is easy to clean up, has some kind of access to an electric point (through a window if need be) and is close to the area of the house that is being worked on. A plasterer will need a water supply and an outside space in which to mix up the plaster, and will then need to carry it to the room being worked on, so the floor may need to be protected. Working with each of the tradesmen to smooth out these details will not only help the project significantly but also make very clear the level of workmanship and care you expect.

Rubbish and cleaning up at the end

Every project generates an extraordinary amount of rubbish. If you are laying a new carpet, the old flooring needs to be disposed of. If you are having a new bathroom installed, the old sanitaryware needs to be removed, as does the packaging for the new. It is helpful to be able to recycle some of it, as

skips are expensive, but expect to be surprised by the amount of rubbish. It is the project manager's job to organize the removal of rubbish, so discuss with the workmen what they will remove themselves and what needs to go in a skip. Also, don't assume that this all happens towards the end of a project; stripping out the old takes place straight away, so organizing the delivery of the skip could be one of your first tasks.

Neighbours

Even if you think your work won't affect anyone, tell your neighbours what you are doing. It is human nature to feel better if we know what is going on around us, and unless you live miles from anyone there will be vans, skips and probably some noise that will affect your neighbours. Inform them and make sure they have your phone number in case things get too much for them. If your house is connected to your neighbours' you may need to think about party-wall issues, which concern the impact of your work on adjoining properties. You are legally obliged to take this into account, so if your work is sizable or taking place on a wall that you share with your neighbour, take some general advice on the matter before you start the work.

Photos

Take photographs before work starts and regularly during the project. This is not essential, of course, and it is easily overlooked among the many other things to do, but it really is worthwhile. You will be amazed at how quickly you forget the way things looked before.

A final word

Interior-designing your own home should be fun. The design process should be enjoyable and creative, the project should run smoothly and the result should be a triumph, achieving everything you ever hoped for in a home. However, real life is often an awful lot more complicated than that. Be reassured that it is normal to find some elements of the process (or even all elements of the process) difficult. Interior-designing your own home is much harder than doing it for others. I find that I can look objectively at a customer's brief with fresh eyes, enthusiasm and perspective, but designing my own home can have me running round in circles and making classic mistakes that I would never make at work.

I hope that if you follow the advice in this book, the process will go well and be enjoyable, but please don't worry if you make mistakes. Most can be rectified, and by approaching the project methodically you will reduce the number of problems that arise. Remember also that although the process of interior design is inexplicably harder than it should be, that also means that everything you get right will be all the sweeter. I promise you that the more effort you put into it, the better the result will be. Trust your instincts, do your homework, ignore the advice of well-meaning friends, work with your tradesmen and be proud of what you achieve. And enjoy it if you can.

Happy decorating!

All the rooms shown in this book reflect their owners' style and taste; the way they live; the pride, effort and investment they put into their homes; and the overall evolution of the space. These aspects go a long way towards creating a really stylish home.

Interiors books

If you can identify a book or couple of books that represent your style, you are on to a winner because there will be lots of inspiration in one place for you. It is worth browsing for books in a shop rather than buying online, so that you can be sure what you have chosen is for you. Here I recommend a handful of books that I use a lot when I am designing for other people, but there are so many great interiors books out there that I could recommend 100 and still think of more.

American Farmhouses:
Country Style and Design
Leah Rosch
London (Simon & Schuster) 2002

This book is so beautifully presented that even if your style is not rooted in the country, you will pick up some ideas. It draws on the look of the early American settlers, who created their homes from local materials and initiated design traditions that are still popular today. The look is simple, functional, individual and very stylish – traditional Shaker meets Martha Stewart – and can be used just as well in a modern flat as in a classic American farmhouse.

Contemporary Chic
Rozemarijn de Witte and Hotze Eisma
London (Conran Octopus) 1997

I have owned this book for many years, and I keep coming back to it for ideas. It is full of comfortable, relaxed, carefully thought-through interiors, all with a contemporary slant but often in a period setting. It is very useful for anyone undertaking a project, and there really is something for everyone in its pages.

Creative Homes:
Inside the Private Worlds
of Australia's Stylemakers
Karen McCartney (ed.)
Sydney (Harper Collins) 2005

The Australian homes in this book are all light and airy with a connection to the sun-drenched landscape, but all the interiors could work as well in less equable climates. These eclectic homes are delightful, quirky and comfortable. I have used this book for inspiration on many projects, including my own home.

Dream Homes:
100 Inspirational Interiors
Andreas von Einsiedel and Johanna Thornycroft
London (Merrell) 2006

More Dream Homes:
100 Inspirational Interiors
Andreas von Einsiedel and Johanna Thornycroft
London (Merrell) 2008

I was given *Dream Homes* some years ago, and I have found so much inspiration for my work and my own home that too many pages have been torn out and a new copy has had to be purchased. Both books are great if you are starting to identify your own style and want a wide range to look at.

Glamorous Rooms

Jan Showers

New York (Harry N. Abrams) 2009

One of my clients wanted glamour but had a vast 1960s house that needed everything doing to it. Her style is fairly traditional, but she is a magpie and loves a bit of sheen and shine. This book was the key to finding her style, and I pored over it as I designed her house. I recommend this beautiful book for anyone who likes even a little bit of glamour.

New London Style

Chloe Grimshaw and Ingrid Rasmussen

London (Thames & Hudson) 2009

I am a London girl at heart, and I just adore the urban, trendy, upbeat interiors in this book. It features real (and fabulous) Londoners' homes, and captures the spirit of the city perfectly. It will inspire anyone who loves metropolitan, quirky, cutting-edge interiors with a genuine understanding of heritage.

Perfect English

Ros Byam Shaw and Chris Tubbs

London (Ryland Peters & Small) 2007

For me, this book captures the heart of English decoration: it is not about the considered, beautiful schemes of Henrietta Spencer-Churchill or Nina Campbell but the real look of an English home that has evolved over the years. It encompasses farmhouses, stately homes, town houses and cottages, so if you love a bit of home-grown style, this book is more than worth a look.

Practically Minimal

Maggie Toy

London (Thames & Hudson) 2000

Minimalism does not have to involve huge, bare white spaces. This book presents beautiful, liveable pared-down rooms that focus on light, texture and materials. Its elegant, comfortable interiors are a triumph of both form and function. Even I – an accessories junkie – am inspired by it, and I would urge anyone who loves the minimalist way of life to read it.

Scandinavian Modern

Magnus Englund, Chrystina Schmidt and Andrew Wood

London (Ryland Peters & Small) 2003

I love the look of retro and this book is my guilty pleasure. In the 1950s the Scandinavians embraced a new, modern style that became very popular elsewhere, and many designers whom we now think of as embodying retro style were Scandinavian. This book breaks the look down into its elements, and shows how it can suit any property, from a country house to a city flat.

Shoestring Chic: Extraordinary Style for Less

Gail Abbott and Mark Scott

London (Hearst) 2004

Gail Abbott lives and breathes the art of shabby, shoestring chic, and this book is written from her heart. This book is about understanding the style – from seaside influence to vintage Swedish and French antiques – so thoroughly that pieces picked up from a charity shop, flea market or car boot sale anywhere in the world will look a million dollars when they are installed at home.

Interiors magazines

Magazines are great source of inspiration, and I use them all the time in my design work. I love to bring them back from my travels, because, although the world is increasingly international, people still live in very different ways. Styles are different between countries, not to mention continents, and I find it eye-opening to look at the way other homes are designed. When I approach a new brief, I look at magazines to give my clients inspiration for the style of their home, and it speeds up the process dramatically if I can find early on the magazines that will be right for the project.

Architectural Digest
Beautifully presented and spanning architecture, interiors and gardens, this magazine is always an inspiring read. It contains little 'how-to' information, but consult it to see amazing houses from around the world and a host of celebrity homes.

Country Living
If your idea of heaven is a country kitchen with the door thrown open and a chicken wandering past, look no further. The country look is not my personal style, but I love this magazine because of the beautiful houses it shows and the excellent advice it gives. It always inspires me and makes me long for the next country-house project.

Elle Decoration
This is definitely one of the more contemporary magazines, and has a real eye for contemporary design, quirky interiors and modern architecture. It includes an excellent reference section and is invaluable for getting ideas, finding suppliers and keeping up with the latest in the design world.

Homes & Gardens
This magazine is my personal favourite as it is always stuffed full of liveable homes, from traditional country style to very modern. It contains lots of information and tips on where to buy, and also features gardens and very good recipes.

House Beautiful
This very accessible, balanced magazine has a good mix of real home makeovers and inspirational style shoots, with a focus on the homeowners and the stories behind the projects. You won't find anything too contemporary, but the featured houses are reliably good. The magazine also has an excellent curated list of new products, and the lifestyle section champions home-based businesses as well as covering gardens and food.

House & Garden
A smart magazine with lots of impressive yet inviting and inspirational homes, and good advice and contacts. A similar read to *Homes & Gardens*, it is not bound to a certain look but covers the whole range of tastes and styles.

Ideal Home

Although the homes it presents are not as cutting-edge or design-focused as those in some other magazines, *Ideal Home* is full of useful information and practical advice. Its supplier contacts section is accessible rather than expensive and designer-based, so it is useful for finding products to fit your personal style.

Living etc

This is a feast of ideas that presents the most stylish of contemporary, vintage, retro and ultra-chic designer homes. It features really aspirational homes in an accessible and informative way. It also has a useful suppliers section, which tends to echo the style of the magazine.

Martha Stewart Living

Covering everything homely, from interior design to cooking and practical craft ideas, this magazine is beautifully styled and photographed. Although the featured interiors are incredibly desirable, they are also easily achievable, which means you will get lots of ideas.

The World of Interiors

Quirky, eccentric and at the cutting edge of interior design, this magazine features interiors of all kinds, from a Moroccan riad to a celebrity home in Los Angeles. It is not for the nervous or those keen to stick to the mainstream, but anyone thinking about their interiors should glance at least once at it, if only while browsing the newsagent's shelves.

Interiors websites

The internet is a wonderful source of inspiration and a great help when I am looking for new products. These are just a few of the sites I use as a starting point for finding reliable manufacturers, suppliers and craftsmen.

asid.org

The American Society of Interior Designers has a fantastic Product Finder tool on its website, allowing you to search not only by product or service but also by area. Because it has been designed by the society for the use of interior-design professionals, the content is current and of high quality.

biid.org.uk

The British Institute of Interior Design is the industry body for interior designers in the United Kingdom, and provides a database of suppliers and partners on its website. The list is not exhaustive, as it contains only those suppliers that have registered with the institute, but it is a high-quality one and is well worth a look. It features high-end companies, rather than the mainstream brands.

dcch.co.uk

The Design Centre Chelsea Harbour is a collective of showrooms in London housing some of the best interior-design suppliers. It will lead you to excellent companies with fantastic products, but – as it is quite specialist – it is not exhaustive and does not cover mainstream brands.

thehousedirectory.com

This great website simply lists interiors suppliers in easy-to-use categories, with good contact details and direct links to their websites. Because suppliers pay to be listed, you can be sure not only that they are established companies, but also that they are listed in the most appropriate category. I use this site all the time.

mydeco.com

This site offers a mass of information on many aspects of home design, and lists thousands of suppliers and products. You will need to set aside some time to find what you are after, but there is a wealth of content so you are bound to come across plenty to interest you.

Directory

Lighting and technology

Astro
astrolighting.co.uk

Astro stocks a very good-quality, versatile range of contemporary light fittings and always seems to have just the right piece for the job. It also carries a good range of bathroom lighting, which can be difficult to find elsewhere.

Baulogic
baulogic.com

Designer and installer of electrical automation systems, including lighting, access, security, entertainment, temperature control and data networking, in homes and commercial buildings. Provides very clever systems that I have no doubt we will all expect in our homes in the future.

Bella Figura
bella-figura.com

Beautiful light fittings in both contemporary and traditional styles. These are dramatic investment pieces, so think of them as works of art.

Heathfield
heathfield.co.uk

Creative, high-end table, floor, wall and ceiling lights that make a statement, and a great range of well-made lampshades. All designs can be customized, which is particularly useful for getting the size of lamps and shades right for your scheme.

Jim Lawrence
jim-lawrence.co.uk

A fantastic range of traditional lighting that is hard to beat for classic interiors. Has great designs in a good range of finishes, from antique brass to highly polished nickel; also produces classic door furniture and other home accessories.

John Cullen
johncullenlighting.co.uk

This specialist in home lighting design offers a full design service and also has a fantastic range of light fittings. The London showroom is worth a visit just for its lighting effects.

Louis Poulsen
louispoulsen.com

An iconic Scandinavian lighting design company that is best known in domestic interiors for the beautiful PH5 light of the 1950s, which is a design classic. The company still has a wonderful range that celebrates great design.

Art and accessories

Graham and Green
grahamandgreen.co.uk

An excellent range of fun and imaginative furniture, accessories, gifts and more. It is hard to visit the shop or website and not be at least tempted by something from the extensive range.

Lexington
lexingtoncompany.com

Gorgeous, usable home accessories with a distinctly New England feel. Bedding, blankets and throws, cushions, tableware and towels are at the core of the range, and four new collections each year keep everything up-to-date.

Lynne Strover Gallery
strovergallery.co.uk

A wonderful art gallery that finds and promotes great British contemporary artists. Worth a visit not only for the fantastic art but also for the beautiful gallery itself, which is featured earlier in this book (pp. 42–43).

Marimekko
marimekko.com

This Finnish company works with a wide range of designers to collate a remarkable collection of fabrics, home accessories and clothing. Its desirable products couple bright colours and simple styles with great design.

Melin Tregwynt
melintregwynt.co.uk

A wonderful company that designs and manufactures home furnishings and clothing in Welsh wool. Its traditional and modern designs in beautiful colours include blankets, throws, cushions and fabrics for upholstery.

Niki Jones
niki-jones.co.uk

A unique and delightful range of furnishings and accessories carefully sourced from around the world. There are bold patterns and strong but tasteful colours in abundance, and the pieces work well individually or all together, so it is easy to get carried away.

The Rug Company
therugcompany.info

Exquisite rugs that are handmade, normally to order, from designs by some of the best designers in the world. These are heirlooms of the future, being both made to last and desirable enough to be cherished.

Furniture

Chelsea Textiles
chelseatextiles.com

Best known for its exquisite fabrics and cushions, Chelsea Textiles also produces a lovely range of furniture with good designs and colour palettes. Pieces are grouped into three ranges – Gustavian, Mid-Century Modern and Vintage Lacquer – so there is something for everyone.

George Smith
georgesmith.com

Classic upholstered furniture beautifully crafted to traditional designs. These pieces are designed to last, not just in terms of durability but also in style, and are amazingly comfortable.

Gotham
gothamnottinghill.com

A discerning collection of furniture, lighting, rugs and accessories, with good design at its heart. Flavours of art deco and mid-century modern are in evidence, although low-key chic is the overriding message.

Ligne Roset

ligne-roset.com

Contemporary, edgy furniture from a wide variety of designers in a range of styles, fabrics and sizes. Also produces lighting, rugs and accessories.

Lloyd Loom

lloydloom.co.uk

This historic company makes furniture from paper and wire using a process that results in very durable and robust pieces. The stylish designs encompass both traditional and contemporary looks in a wide range of colours.

Lombok

lombok.co.uk

Handmade furniture in a range of styles and solid woods. Pieces are built to last, and the designs are simple but well proportioned, making them useful in many different types of scheme.

Paint

Designers Guild

designersguild.com

Tricia Guild is a colour genius, and this is reflected in her fabrics and paint range. She draws inspiration from hot climates, particularly India, a fact that is evident in her sharp, clean range of paints. The colours are bold and beautiful, and the neutrals are clear and light.

Farrow & Ball

farrow-ball.com

Farrow & Ball is a master of colour and produces great paint. The firm is perhaps best known for the stylish historic-house look, but the range also works wonderfully well in contemporary urban interiors.

Fired Earth

firedearth.com

Fired Earth is a core range of paints in any interior designer's palette because it offers an up-to-date, interesting twist on a classic collection of colours. There is also a range of true period colours created in collaboration with the National Trust in the United Kingdom.

Little Greene

littlegreene.com

Great-quality paints in a punchy range of colours. The paints are highly pigmented for a great depth of colour, even in neutrals.

Paint Library

paintlibrary.co.uk

This is a truly gorgeous range, with a very versatile and likeable selection of colours. The architectural collection, particularly, is one of the most useful paint ranges I have come across, and one I use all the time.

Sanderson

sanderson-uk.com

A larger collection of paint than I would generally recommend, with more than 1300 colours, but very beautiful and usable. There are some great neutrals but also a lot of good mid-range colours.

Zoffany

zoffany.com

I first used Zoffany paints for more contemporary projects, but have found that they also work well in smart country homes. This is a very grown-up range of paints, with excellent urban neutrals and some fantastic deeper colours.

Wallpaper

Andrew Martin
andrewmartin.co.uk

A fun and innovative range that is strong on design. Many of the papers use *trompe l'œil* to create the illusion of a bookcase or shutters; all are witty and clever.

Cole & Son
cole-and-son.com

A historic company producing some of the finest wallpapers around, with an extensive range of both traditional and contemporary designs. Specializes in all types of printing, so it can make bespoke wallpaper when required.

Colefax and Fowler
colefax.com

A classic British company that produces beautiful wallpapers and fabrics. Essential for traditional or country wallpapers, although the range is wide, so don't be put off if your taste is more modern.

Dedar
dedar.com

Mainly contemporary designs or modern takes on traditional patterns, in subtle colours with lots of texture. The gorgeous

wallpapers coordinate perfectly with Dedar's fabrics and trims.

Ralph Lauren
ralphlauren.com

Traditional yet up-to-date wallpapers from a design genius. As are all Ralph Lauren's home-furnishing products, these are really elegant and desirable. Distributed through Designers Guild in the United Kingdom.

Turner Pocock Cazalet
turnerpocockcazalet.co.uk

A small but beautiful range of unusual wallpaper by the designer Catherine Cazalet, with a modern feel and a clever colour palette. See one of the company's papers inside the pendant light on p. 180.

Flooring and tiles

Crucial Trading
crucial-trading.com

Fantastic for wool carpets, but also supplies a great range of sisal, coir, seagrass and jute. The rugs are very smart and good value for money, and you can select your size, type, border and piping online for an instant quotation.

Jacaranda Carpets
jacarandacarpets.com

If you want to feel real luxury under your feet, Jacaranda's handmade wool and silk rugs and carpets may be just the thing. There is a good selection of colours and finishes, and a bespoke service.

Karndean
karndean.co.uk
karndean.com

One look at these floors will change your mind about vinyl. I have a Karndean imitation parquet floor in my office, and it is indestructible, waterproof, easy to clean and indistinguishable from the real thing.

Original Style

originalstyle.com

A beautiful range of traditional tiles, with wonderful colours and eye-catching decoration. Also supplies Victorian floor tiles to original designs.

Roger Oates

rogeroates.com

Designs and manufactures some of the very best stair runners available. They are stylish and hardwearing, and are suited to both traditional and contemporary interiors.

Ryalux

ryalux.com

Very good-quality twist and velvet carpets in a great range of colours. Ryalux carpets are a core part of many of my design schemes, as they offer a balance of luxury and practicality. There is also a colour-matching service if you cannot find exactly the shade you need.

World's End Tiles

worldsendtiles.co.uk

A wide selection of tiles for modern and contemporary interiors; also great for stylish neutral tiles in lots of different sizes and colours. Some wonderful mosaics and glass tiles, too, if you want to make a statement.

Bathroom fittings

Crosswater

crosswater.co.uk

A great range of bathroom taps, shower heads and valves, and bathroom accessories from a variety of designers. All products are very usable and well made.

Duravit

duravit.com

A wide range of high-quality products, great for simple, contemporary bathrooms, created by such renowned designers as Philippe Starck and Norman Foster.

Imperial Bathrooms

imperialbathrooms.com

A desirable range of classic roll-top baths, beautiful taps and stylish washstands. Understated, functional and timeless, they are the perfect choice for period bathrooms and cloakrooms.

Lefroy Brooks

lefroybrooks.co.uk

Supplies some of the most stylish bathroom fittings available, specializing in Victorian and art deco designs but with a gorgeous modern range, too. Understated classics that will add glamour and sophistication to any bathroom.

Majestic

majesticshowers.com

High-quality, well-designed shower enclosures that feel very solid. Most requirements can be met from the many different sizes and configurations in the range, but there is also a bespoke service.

Samuel Heath

samuel-heath.co.uk
samuel-heath.com

Great for both classic and modern bathroom accessories, taps and showers. Also designs and manufactures lovely door and window furniture and fittings. This historic company has built its name on design and quality, and that is evident in its products.

Kitchens

Bulthaup

bulthaup.com
Modern, clean-lined kitchens that are sleek and functional and make a statement. Good quality and cutting-edge design.

Corian

dupont.com/corian

Corian is a synthetic material that is great for work surfaces. It can be moulded to curved surfaces, even to create a sink, and can be of any size or depth. It also comes in a huge range of colours, so the design options are endless.

Durat

durat.com

A polyester-based worktop product that can also be used to make baths, sinks and furniture. It looks great, comes in any colour you want (although the seventy standard colours are a good starting point), is totally recyclable and is made from 30% recycled materials itself.

Miele

miele.com

High-quality household appliances that are right up to date with technology. They are not cheap, but once you have had a Miele appliance you won't want anything else.

Plain English

plainenglishdesign.co.uk

A traditional joinery company that designs and makes beautiful kitchens using skilled cabinet-makers and great attention to detail. These kitchens are designed to last a lifetime.

Schüller

schueller.de

Modern contemporary kitchens in a range of prices, styles and colours. Good design and quality, and flexible unit sizes so that you can create a bespoke look rather than having to choose from what is available.

Fabrics

G.P. & J. Baker
gpjbaker.com

Wonderful traditional, high-quality fabrics in beautiful colours. A fantastic range with lots of options, from the more affordable to the reassuringly expensive.

Caitlin Wilson Textiles
cwdtextiles.com

A delightful collection of fabrics and accessories from a very talented designer. Wilson's Californian roots are in evidence in her collection, although her designs would look good anywhere.

Kravet
kravet.com

A long-established family business that has a range of superb fabrics of its own and also represents other designers, including Jonathan Adler, Barbara Barry and Michael Weiss. In addition, it supplies ranges of furniture, carpets and trimmings that are all worth a look.

Lewis & Wood
lewisandwood.co.uk

These fabrics and wallpapers are based on classic British designs, and offer a clever mix of old-world charm and an up-to-date look. A wide range of sporting and character fabric as well as more traditional checks, damasks and plains.

Marvic Textiles
marvictextiles.co.uk

Elegant and glamorous textiles, with ranges of woven fabric and delicate toile and a fantastic selection of upholstery fabric.

Osborne & Little
osborneandlittle.com

A brilliant range of fabric, wallpaper and trimmings in modern, innovative designs based on traditional style and simplicity. This company also produces and distributes Nina Campbell's gorgeous designs.

Pierre Frey
pierrefrey.com

The embodiment of French style and flair – elegant and luxurious and in fabulous colour combinations. The best range of illustrative fabrics available,

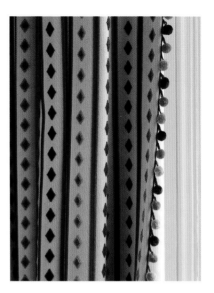

drawing inspiration from history and around the world.

St Judes
stjudesfabrics.co.uk

A wonderful company that works with a range of artists and printmakers for an eclectic and playful range of excellent-quality fabric and wallpaper. There is nothing else like it on the market.

Zimmer + Rohde
zimmer-rohde.com

One of the first fabric companies I ever worked with, and still one of my favourites. Designs with a modern feel and a nod to tradition; the colour combinations are always exciting.

Fittings, Hardware and Ironmongery

Clement Browne
clementbrowne.co.uk

Supplies and fits good-quality, made-to-order shutters in any colour you like. There is nothing smarter than window shutters if they are used the right way, and they are great for providing privacy if your windows are overlooked.

Elfa
elfa.com

A simple but ingenious storage system from a company that has been around since the 1940s. The product can be customized to maximize your storage space.

Häfele
hafele.com

A vast collection of furniture fittings and ironmongery. The company supplies to trade only, but find the item you need on their website and you will be able to purchase it through one of the distributors.

Holloways of Ludlow
hollowaysofludlow.com

A wide range of door furniture and ironmongery as well as many other items, in both contemporary and traditional styles. Just about every finish you could require, including metal, wood, glass, ceramic and leather.

Willow & Stone
willowandstone.co.uk

Great for doorknobs and handles, front-door furniture, hooks, household goods, kitchen and bathroom accessories, and more. A well-put-together collection of products in mainly period styles.

Antiques and salvage

Alfies Antique Market
alfiesantiques.com

This arcade makes a great day out: a fabulous treasure trove of homewares, fashion, jewellery and lots more from over 100 dealers.

John Beazor Antiques
johnbeazorantiques.co.uk

Specializes in eighteenth- and early nineteenth-century furniture, clocks and decorative pieces. Now run by the great-grandson of the founder, this company has a reputation for quality.

LASSCO
lassco.co.uk

The London Architectural Salvage Supply Company is a leader in architectural reclaim and always has a wonderful selection of stock.

Retrouvius
retrouvius.com

An ever-changing selection of architectural salvage. Stock is often from old commercial buildings, so there are normally some amazing finds.

Sotheby's

sothebys.com

One of the largest auctioneers in the world, with many locations worldwide. It may not be for all to buy from, but you can't fail to be inspired by the auctions.

Stretton Antiques Market

36 Sandford Avenue, Church Stretton, Shropshire SY6 6BH

A varied selection of antiques and quirky finds, from wardrobes to china, spread over many floors of a fascinating old building. Also sells supplies for restoring furniture, and there is even a cafe.

Willingham Auctions

willinghamauctions.com

Buying at auction is a very special way to shop, but great fun if you approach it in the right way. This auction house makes a great day out; if you are serious about buying, make sure you visit to view all the stock before the auction itself.

General

Angel + Blume Interior Design

angelandblume.com

My interior-design company, based in Cambridge, England. The website has details of our projects and courses, a blog and information about our books.

Joa Studholme, Colour Consultant

farrow-ball.com

Joa is an amazing colour consultant with expertise in both residential and commercial properties. She will advise on colours for your home from the beautiful Farrow & Ball paint range, and can be contacted through the company.

Vitra Design Museum

design-museum.de

One of the best design museums in the world, with an extensive collection of furniture and interior-design-related artefacts, including an amazing collection of chairs.

Index

Acknowledgements

First published in 2013 by Merrell Publishers, London and New York

Merrell Publishers Limited
81 Southwark Street
London SE1 0HX

merrellpublishers.com

British Library Cataloguing in Publication Data:
A catalogue record for this book is available from the British Library.

ISBN 978-1-8589-4591-0

Produced by Merrell Publishers Limited
Designed by Nicola Bailey
Project-managed by Rosanna Lewis
Indexed by Hilary Bird

Printed and bound in China

I should like to thank all the owners of the houses that appear in this book, who were kind enough to let us photograph their homes (an intrusion in more ways than just the chaos we create on the day). Some are customers of my studio, Angel + Blume, and some are friends who have had no interior design assistance at all, but all have a tremendous sense of their own taste and preferences. Because of that, their homes are truly beautiful. Thank you to the whole team at Merrell, who saw the potential in this book when others didn't and provided invaluable expertise and guidance through the long process of producing the material. Finally, and most importantly, an interiors book is nothing without beautiful, inspirational photography: my heartfelt thanks go to Simon Whitmore for the skill and effort he put into every image in this book.

The author and publisher are grateful to Andreas von Einsiedel for the use of his photography on pp. 20–22, and to Plain English for the use of its advertisement on p. 22.

9 781858 945910

Acknowledgements

First published in 2013 by Merrell Publishers, London
and New York

Merrell Publishers Limited
81 Southwark Street
London SE1 0HX

merrellpublishers.com

British Library Cataloguing in Publication Data:
A catalogue record for this book is available from the
British Library.

ISBN 978-1-8589-4591-0

Produced by Merrell Publishers Limited
Designed by Nicola Bailey
Project-managed by Rosanna Lewis
Indexed by Hilary Bird

Printed and bound in China

I should like to thank all the owners of the houses that
appear in this book, who were kind enough to let us
photograph their homes (an intrusion in more ways than
just the chaos we create on the day). Some are customers
of my studio, Angel + Blume, and some are friends who
have had no interior design assistance at all, but all have
a tremendous sense of their own taste and preferences.
Because of that, their homes are truly beautiful. Thank you
to the whole team at Merrell, who saw the potential in this
book when others didn't and provided invaluable expertise
and guidance through the long process of producing the
material. Finally, and most importantly, an interiors book
is nothing without beautiful, inspirational photography:
my heartfelt thanks go to Simon Whitmore for the skill
and effort he put into every image in this book.

The author and publisher are grateful to Andreas von
Einsiedel for the use of his photography on pp. 20–22, and
to Plain English for the use of its advertisement on p. 22.